Revolutionizing Christian Stewardship

for the 21st Century:

Lessons from Copernicus

Dan R. Dick

DISCIPLESHIP RESOURCES

P.O. BOX 840 • NASHVILLE, TN 37202

ISBN 0-88177-212-7

Library of Congress Catalog Card No. 96-72437

DR212

CONTENTS

ACKNOWLEDGMENTS

This book is the result of a number of requests from colleagues, friends, and seminar participants who expressed a desire to see these ideas in print. I offer a deep appreciation to the many people across the country who talked with me at length about these ideas. I have included quotations from many individuals, with their permission, though no direct references are footnoted in order to preserve promised anonymity. Names and locations have been altered for the sake of confidentiality wherever personal quotations are indicated. This book is made readable by the inclusion of so many perspectives other than my own.

Special thanks is also extended to Herb Mather, Don Joiner, Craig Miller, Henk Pieterse, and my wife, Nancy Dick, for their support, comments, and encouragement along the way.

Last, thanks to Dr. Neill Q. Hamilton, who taught me not to get so caught up in the details that I neglect to look at the big picture. His systems thinking approach to the Christian faith will forever shape my ministry and my growth as a disciple and steward.

PREFACE

More than one local church finance committee has had a member who regularly stated the mantra that "the church is a business and needs to be run like one." Think of the implications of such a statement! Any secular business that forgets its mission is in deep trouble. Although a secular business needs to produce a profit to stay in business, the profit is not the mission. There must be something the business does that adds value to people and to society—something that people desire.

In that sense, the church is like a business. It does not exist in order to exist. Its legitimacy comes from knowing *why* it exists and from marshaling its spiritual, human, and temporal resources to fulfill its primary task. The church is a steward when it is faithful to its mission. When the church tries to *become* the mission rather than to act as a *steward* of the mission, it has forfeited its reason for being.

In 1992, Bill Clinton ran for president on the slogan, "It's the economy, stupid." This book has a clear, simple, and parallel theme, "It's the mission, steward!" Dan Dick's reasoned arguments and clear appeals help redeem the word *stewardship* from its present confusion within the church.

Over the past twenty or thirty years, a creeping evolution has been distorting a good biblical word. Churches have moved away from an understanding of the steward as one who responds to the invitation to use all that God has provided in ways that would please God. Stewardship has been redefined as a financial campaign or some other method of extracting funds from reluctant givers. While the church skewed the definition of stewardship into *fundraising,* the secular world discovered the biblical meaning of the steward as *manager* of all we have and all we are. This book is a cry to the church to reclaim the biblical understanding of stewardship.

I invite you as church leaders, both lay and clergy, to use this book as an opportunity to reexamine your understanding of Christian stewardship. In these pages, you will discover viable alternatives to a church being driven by structure or by budgets.

Enter into the freedom.

Herb Mather
General Board of Discipleship
Nashville, Tennessee

Looking with new eyes:
Are we ready for change?

n 1543, Polish astronomer Nicolaus Copernicus presented a challenging and provocative picture to the world of the sixteenth century when he published *De Revolutionibus Orbium Coelestium* (On the Revolutions of the Heavenly Spheres). The vision he shared was that of a solar system: a universe that revolved around the sun, rather than around the earth. To our world, poised on the threshold of the twenty-first century, the idea of a solar system is ordinary and has been proved scientifically again and again. To the world of the sixteenth century, the idea of a sun-centered universe was strange, mysterious, and even threatening. For Copernicus to make such an assertion was to risk his life. New ideas were not well received in Europe in the 1500's.

A deeply religious and devout man, Copernicus approached the study of the heavens with great respect and deep awe. It was from the center of his Christian faith that he committed his life to the pursuit of truth through science. Copernicus offered his discoveries to the world and to the church with a sense of expectancy. He believed that he would be commended for his contributions to the understanding of the universe.

Fierce debate followed the publication of *De Revolutionibus*. The church denounced the Copernican theory as heretical and satanic. Other astronomers, though believing the validity of the solar system model, feared for their lives and remained mute. Copernicus, failing in health, was unable to enter the fray. His choice was to hold fast to the centrality of the sun, regardless of the popular opinion of the church that all things revolved around the earth. While Copernicus lay near death, a contemporary of his, Andrew Osiander, defused the debate by rewriting the introduction to the great astronomer's manuscript. Osiander wrote:

> And as far as hypotheses go, let no one expect anything in the way
> of certainty from astronomy, since astronomy can offer us nothing

certain, lest, if anyone take as true that which has been constructed for another use, he go away from this discipline a bigger fool than when he came to it.[1]

With this disclaimer intact, *De Revolutionibus* received papal approbation. ■

Loren Mead, in his book, *The Once and Future Church*,[2] claims that today's church is emerging from the Age of Christendom, the era of the institutional church. The Age of Christendom stretches back to the dawn of the institutional church at the close of the Apostolic Age in the third and fourth centuries. The age that is currently dawning is as yet unformed, and what we will become as the people of God through Jesus Christ is not clear. Within this thesis, the sixteenth century stands as a turning point, where the infallibility of the church—the cornerstone of Christendom—was challenged.

The solar system controversy was not the only challenge to the church in the sixteenth century. The seeds were being sown for the Protestant Reformation at the same time that Nicolaus Copernicus was "reinventing" the universe. The Protestant Reformation and the postulation of a solar system make sense today, and their validity is obvious; but it was not always so. Change is difficult, and when the change demands first that people have to admit that they are wrong, it is sometimes nearly impossible.

Copernicus opened a gateway that reoriented humankind to reality. The church, heart and voice of the reality of the day, long held to the centrality of the earth. The earth was God's crowning achievement in all creation. Humankind was the jewel on the crown. The church was the caretaker of the sacred truth, and all was right with the world. A place for everything and everything in its place. Nothing could shake the ground upon which the Christian church was founded. It was not wise to question the fundamental teachings of the church.

Copernicus, and those like him, literally risked their lives to offer new ideas and challenge old ones. Nearly one century later, when Galileo confirmed the solar center theory of Copernicus, he incurred the wrath of the church and was summoned to Rome where he recanted his scientific beliefs to save his own life. The damage, however, had been done. Galileo discovered four of Jupiter's moons and observed the way they revolved around the huge planet. After recording their phases for almost a year, Galileo noted that Mercury, Venus, and Mars also went through phases, indicating that they did not revolve around the earth as did the moon, but orbited the sun instead. What Copernicus initiated, Galileo engaged; and from the mid-seventeenth century onward, science and religion embarked on a turbulent journey.

Reality is a funny thing. The reality of the sixteenth century was that the world was flat—until it was not flat anymore. The reality was that the earth was the center of the universe—until it was not the center anymore. The reality was that human beings could not fly—until they could. Reality, which we hold as changeless and absolute, is constantly changing. In fact, it appears that the only true, absolute reality is change. Even as changeless as God is, God is continually changing our reality. The biblical narrative is a panoramic view of the ways in which God's people respond in the face of change. As people adapt and evolve through their faith and faithfulness, they succeed. As people harden and grow inflexible, they break and are crushed. So it is with churches.

The current reality of many of our churches is "change or perish." Holding fast to effective and meaningful processes, structures, and programs of the past seems wise; but perhaps it is not. "We-have-never-done-it-that-way-before" churches are complaining of aches, pains, and a decided lack of energy. Fear of losing "what we have" has replaced enthusiasm for "what we might become." Our ability to go forth and make disciples is limited by our need to stay home and care for the maintenance and survival needs of the local church.

The world is changing at lightning speed. How does the church respond? The response usually takes one of two forms. The church defines itself either by what it has been, adopting a conventional position and digging in its heels; or it defines itself in relation to its mission into the twenty-first century. One approach places the institution of the church at the center and asks, "What do people need to do in order to be part of what we are?" The second approach asks, "What does the church need to be to connect people to God through Jesus Christ?" The first concept places the *church* at the center, while the second recognizes *God* as the center. With the church at the center, we create *members*. With God at the center, we create *disciples* and *stewards*.

Today's church faces a crisis similar to the church in the day of Copernicus. The leadership of the sixteenth-century church viewed itself as caretaker of the sacred truth. That truth held that the church stood at the very pinnacle of all creation. If the universe revolved around the earth, then the earth revolved around the church. In our day, the church has come once more to hold center stage. Somehow, the institutional church threatens to replace God at the center of our faith. The institution of the church—the means to the end of faithful discipleship in order to transform the world into God's kingdom—threatens to become an end in itself. A great deal of our time, energy, and resources are channeled not into the work of the church, but directly into the preservation of the institution. The challenge today is to awaken to the fact that the church is not the center of the Christian universe—Christ is.

This book focuses on Christian stewardship. Many of the principles discussed here could apply equally to other aspects of the church. However, stewardship provides an appropriate illustration. More than most practices in the church, stewardship has experienced a shift away from its true meaning—to support a process of growth for Christian disciples—to a distorted meaning of supporting the needs of the institution, primarily through funding. Ultimately, stewardship is not so much what we do, but a way of identifying who we are.

The swing in focus from the need of the believer to support the church as an institution to the need of the believer to participate fully in the mission and ministry of the body of Christ has positive effects. Terry Gates, a young pastor in Wisconsin, says, "I never heard stewardship defined as identity; not in Sunday school, not in seminary, nowhere. I always thought something was missing. I always thought that being a disciple was a compelling start, but not the whole picture. Becoming a 'servant of Christ and a steward of the gospel' filled in some missing pieces in my ministry. Now I know the reason I became a disciple. Stewardship, real stewardship, finally helped me know what it means to be a Christian."

The goal of Christian stewardship is life-changing transformation. God has called us to be faithful stewards. What we give to and through the church emerges from who we are. Though not by any means a new understanding of Christian stewardship, this is a radically different view from what many churches now teach. What would happen to our churches if this transformational understanding of Christian stewardship became the norm? What might be the result if the emphasis of stewardship shifted from "doing" to "being"?

Barry, a participant in a spiritual gifts discovery workshop in Kansas, asked me, "How do we know that your approach is going to be any better than what we're already doing?" This is a fair question. The answer that was offered then is offered now: "There are no guarantees, but the pertinent question to ask ourselves is, 'Is what we are currently calling stewardship in the majority of our churches yielding the results we need to grow and faithfully participate in the mission and ministry of Jesus Christ?'" Wherever I asked that question, the answer was unanimous: "What we are currently doing is not working, or it could be working a lot better." When what we do ceases to yield the results we need, then it is time to do something different.

Ezra Earl Jones, general secretary of the General Board of Discipleship of The United Methodist Church, often quotes a fundamental principle of total quality management: "The system is designed for the results it is getting." (Or, as Yogi Berra is rumored to have replied in the 1960's when asked why he kept changing the New York Mets batting order every day, "When you do what you done, you get what you got.") The current understanding of Christian stewardship in most churches is not enabling the community of faith to thrive and prosper. Something is wrong.

It takes only a quick look to see that there are many high-quality stewardship programs available. There are many well-written, biblically-based books, campaigns, and resources to assist churches in the work of Christian stewardship. Developing new and improved resources is not the answer. What we already have is more than adequate. Excellent sermons on giving, tithing, pledging, and serving have been, and continue to be, delivered. Good seed is sown, but the condition of the soil is questionable. To speak in systems language, we have dedicated most of our time to tinkering with inputs in order to change outputs, without ever questioning the processing system itself.

A famous pizza maker near a large college campus successfully served the community for years. A smaller restaurant opened and offered free delivery. Its business soared, seriously hurting the profit of the long-standing eatery. The famous pizza maker began changing ingredients, making new crusts, fillings, and toppings. He renovated the dining room, he added to the menu, he offered specials, but he refused to deliver his pizzas to the campus. He is now working for the once-smaller restaurant. His pizza parlor went bankrupt. Times changed, and the customers were looking for something new. The quality of the pizza was never in question. The outputs desired had very little to do with the inputs received. It was the system that was the issue.[3]

The same is true of Christian stewardship. We have wonderful input in the form of quality materials and loving fellowships. We desire transformed lives as our output. It is our "throughput," our system of transformation, that needs to be examined. The old ways may not work as effectively anymore. Merely tinkering with the tools and resources, working diligently to improve what is already good enough, misses the point. Annual financial campaigns; time, talent, and gifts surveys; second-mile giving appeals; church bazaars (bordering on the bizarre); and the like are remnants of a bygone day. They have all served the church well in their time and in their place. In fact, there are still times and places where these tools can yield marvelous results, but changing times demand changing methods. To receive new results, we need to employ new approaches.

The worlds of science and religion collided in the sixteenth century. With the revelation by Copernicus that the earth revolved around the sun, the world was forever changed. The sun and the earth did not change. Nothing occurred except a shift in perception, the emergence of a new paradigm. What Copernicus conjectured to be true had always been true. As scientists of the twentieth century have pointed out, Copernicus did not invent this concept. Cave paintings, tens of thousands of years old, depict the earth revolving around the sun. Philosophers of the second century B.C.E. (before the common era) debated the centrality of the earth to the cosmos. Copernicus did not "invent" the solar system: what he did was open a new way of looking at reality. Opening a new way of looking at our reality is the intention of this book.

Christian stewardship begins with God at the center. When stewardship revolves around any other center, it is misconceived. The institution of the church is an inadequate substitute for the incarnate body of Christ. The church as institution is a *means to the end* of the church as the fellowship of all believers. Stewardship is servanthood to God through the church, not to the church institution. Though this is a subtle distinction, it is significant.

As we begin to think of stewardship in a fundamentally different light, a powerful shift in perspective takes place. First, we see that we exist as an institution to fulfill the mission and purpose of the church as the body of Christ. Second, we are forced to examine our "we-have-always-done-it-that-way-before" practices to chart new maps that better reflect the ever-changing terrain in which our churches find themselves. Third, we realize that stewardship is not primarily concerned with what people give to the institutional church. Rather, it is concerned with managing what we have been given by God and how we respond most appropriately to God's goodness. Last, we reclaim the church as the body of Christ, composed of diverse and gifted people who are growing in their discipleship and sharing their faith throughout the community and the world. Rather than the church being served by its members, the church serves the membership by enabling gifted and called men and women to honor and glorify God in their daily living.

The statistics of most mainline denominations clearly indicate that something is wrong. We are losing members. We are struggling financially. Our attendance is down. Mission giving is on the wane.[4] What worked well in the past is not working today. The time has come to take a serious look not only at what we are doing, but also—more important—at how and why we do what we do. The church stands in a unique position to be a place where God can transform lives. It can be a vehicle through which God can make our world a better place. The church has been given the sacred responsibility to spread the gospel throughout the world. We are stewards of that sacred trust.

Matthew 25:14-30 tells the familiar parable of the talents. Three servants were entrusted with a portion of their master's wealth. Two of the servants used their master's money wisely, and they doubled it in his absence. They returned what they had received, plus a one-hundred percent increase. The third servant hid the money; and when the master returned, the servant gave him only the original amount, nothing more. Those who added something to their trust were rewarded, but the one who added nothing received punishment. The first two servants understood that stewardship meant actively striving to benefit their master. This pleased the master. The third servant played it safe, misunderstanding the meaning of stewardship. It would have been better for this servant to have lost the money in a faithful effort to increase it. Even failure qualifies as faithful stewardship when the best effort is given. Two of the stewards remembered whom they served, and they served their master well. The last steward forgot his purpose, and he failed in his stewardship.

In cases where our stewardship has been ineffective, we have no cause for shame. At least we are trying to do the best we know how. However, when the best we know how is not good enough, it is time to try something new. Just working harder will not be enough; we need to work smarter. Unlike the lazy steward in the parable of the talents, we are trying to be faithful. We strive to be as trustworthy as possible. It is this commitment to faithfulness that will enable us to shift our perspective. Our desire to please God, to hear God say, "Well done, good and faithful steward," is what will allow us to move from the way we have always done things to a new way of doing and being in the world.

Revolutionizing Christian Stewardship for the 21st Century is a call to reorient ourselves in relationship to God and God's church. Chapter 1 addresses the need to focus less on institutional support and more on the need to grow as faithful Christians. Chapter 2 examines what happens when a "stewardship-as-maintaining-the-institution" mindset prevails, and it challenges us to move beyond it. Chapter 3 offers the image of the body of Christ as an alternative to the current institutional focus. Chapter 4 explores how to discern and develop the giftedness of the body of Christ. Chapter 5 discusses a different way to see our congregations in order to be more effective at communicating faithful stewardship. The conclusion presents a brief consideration of the implications of moving from an institutional orientation to a relational body of Christ orientation.

CHAPTER 1

Adrift in space:
Why are we here?

arth was at the center. There was no other possibility. God had ordained that humankind was the jewel of all creation. Men and women had been given dominion over creation. The sun, the moon, and the stars made their daily appearances for the benefit of the earth. The earth existed in the foundation of heaven. On the fringes rested "space" and beyond that— chaos. God held the earth steady at the center. This was the reality of the scientific world of the sixteenth century; yet, not everyone was satisfied. Nicolaus Copernicus saw things differently. He put forth a new way of viewing reality. Many of the mysteries of the world could be answered by just a slight, but significant shift in perspective. If the sun were at the center of the planetary system instead of the earth, then changes in the seasons could be explained. Differences between the hemispheres made sense. The movement of the planets, the constellations, and the appearance and disappearance of comets all entered the realm of the rational. Scientifically, this shift in perspective was considered to be a monumental step forward, but science was not the respected discipline then that it is today. Reality was defined, not by science, but by religion. The church had established the earth as the center, suspended in space, unmoving and immovable, except by the hand of God. It was by faith and by God's revelation that the concept of earth, stationary in space, had come into being. To accept the challenge of Copernicus was to question the church, to question God. Scientific discovery was not a blessing, but a threat. The best and easiest course was to ignore it. So intent was the church on maintaining the understanding of the ages that it made acceptance of Copernican astronomy a capital sin, punishable by death.

While the threat might not be as great, nor the punishment quite so severe, the church today often finds itself facing the same tension caused by a shift in perspective. We have been "adrift in space" for quite some time; and to change our perspective, to face new realities, causes great distress. We assume that "where we are must be where we are supposed to be," and we neglect to evaluate where we are in relation to our call to be God's church. A constant seeking of the will of God is an essential part of faithful stewardship, because it forces us to look outside ourselves to understand where we are and why we are here. The church at rest is not the church alive. We are not merely drifting, but moving toward the fulfillment of a divine calling. Clearly, a vision is necessary to ensure that we will not stagnate and just drift. The church is in a preordained orbit, serving and saving in the name of Christ.

It is imperative that stewards understand what has been entrusted to their care. The first work of Christian stewardship in the church is to create a clear and compelling vision for fulfilling the primary mission to which God calls us. In this chapter, we discuss the basic components of such a vision. ▪

The apostle Paul taught the congregation in Corinth to "think of us in this way, as servants of Christ and stewards of God's mysteries" (1 Corinthians 4:1). Servanthood and stewardship are touchstones for Christian leadership. As church leaders, we serve Christ and manage God's mysteries. The concept of service is fairly widespread throughout the church, but what exactly are the mysteries of God? Can we be faithful stewards of something if we are not sure what that something is?

The *mysteries* that Paul refers to are the basic tenets and practices of the church: baptism and Eucharist; the Crucifixion and the Resurrection; propitiation and grace; and a plethora of other concepts that are common within the church, but quite puzzling to those outside the church. These mysteries are not confusing to the church, but they mystify the uninitiated. To be faithful stewards of the mysteries means to manage well and wisely these tenets and practices in order to honor and glorify God so that the world might be transformed. Therefore, evangelism becomes an act of Christian stewardship as we extend the invitation to others to become part of the body of Christ.

Stewardship and the Church's Primary Task

In The United Methodist Church, we incorporate "God's mysteries" into our definition of the mission of the church. For us, the mission of the church is summed up best in the Great Commission that Jesus gave to his followers in Matthew 28:19a, "Go therefore and make disciples of all nations." This mission helps give focus to the core purpose of the larger Christian church: to transform the world into the kingdom of God. Disciple-making is our primary task in the fulfillment of our work of transformation.[5] The process of our primary task is fourfold: (1) to reach out and receive people into our fellowships; (2) to relate people to God through the gospel and the community of faith; (3) to strengthen and nurture people in their relationship to God and the Christian community; and (4) to send people out into the world to live as transformed and transforming believers in Christ who invite others to join the fellowship; thus completing the circuit and beginning the fourfold process again.

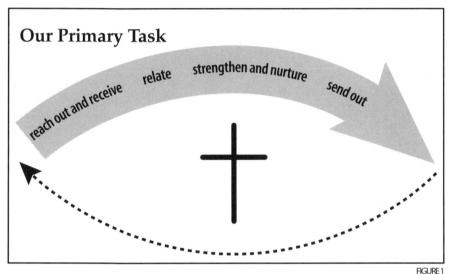

Our Primary Task

reach out and receive · relate · strengthen and nurture · send out

FIGURE 1

Figure 1 illustrates the "flow" of the core process. One problem with this model is that it appears to be linear in that one phase cleanly follows the next. This is not the case. In order to truly be the church, all four phases operate simultaneously. Though a church may display a dominant strength in one of these four areas, no church can survive unless the flow continues throughout the process. Stewardship within the church is the process by which we manage the flow of our core process. Our vision for ministry is incomplete unless it encompasses all four aspects. As one layperson at Hesston United Methodist Church says about her congregation, "We're very strong in relating and nurturing, but very weak in reaching and sending out. We have a vision for our church *inside*, but we have no vision for *outside*." This comment challenges us to consider where the ministry of the church really takes place: inside or outside? The answer, of course, is both, but many churches find that they have a hard time balancing the two. A common criticism of The United Methodist Church is that it has lost its missional identity and has grown complacent, happy to function as an institution with maintenance and survival as the primary reasons for existing. When churches focus on the relating and nurturing aspects of the primary task to the exclusion of reaching out, receiving, and sending out to live as empowered Christians, then the church can become "ingrown." Likewise, a church that builds its identity upon reaching out without adequately relating people to God and nurturing them in their faith will find itself with no one to send out. The primary task and mission of the church is a process, and each aspect flows together with the other aspects to create a healthy system.

An analogy for this flow is an inland body of water. For an aquatic water system to exist, four things must occur. First, there must be a feeder or in-flow system. Fresh water must enter. Second, a settling or clarifying process must take place. This clarifying process clears the water and allows life to exist. Third, there must be a generation phase, during which life processes take place. These processes, while life-enhancing, also soil the water and make a cleaning process necessary. Fourth, a cleaning process must happen, where the water is passed on—an out-flow—which cleanses the system. If any one of these processes breaks down, the entire system eventually fails. Without fresh in-flow, the body of water dries up. Without the clarifying process, no life can exist. Without the third phase, the body of water will grow sterile. Lacking the fourth phase, the water will become brackish and stagnant, and once again the system will be destroyed. There is a delicate balance that must be maintained, and each is intricately tied to the others. The church "flow" is very similar.

As stewards of the church, we have a unique responsibility to discern and pursue a vision for our primary task and to create a working core process. What does each of the phases look like? How do we "manage" this fourfold process of the primary task of the church?

The following simple definition allows us to see ways to apply stewardship to our primary task: "Stewardship is the appreciation and management of resources and opportunities for ministry that God has given us and the maximization of their potential for Christian transformation in the world."

Stewards Reach Out and Receive

Millie T., a delightful woman from Pennsylvania, is a seventy-nine-year member of her Methodist church. She analyzes one of the problems of her congregation this way: "We say we want new members, but we really don't. We participate in our own set of rituals and follow our own traditions; we talk to the people we know; and we celebrate the lives of the existing members. Newcomers must be bewildered when they try to figure us out, and no one from the inside ever reaches out to the people on the outside. We all like our church very much. We are afraid to see it change." These profound words identify a rudimentary obstacle to faithful stewardship of the church: we value what *is* over what *might be*. The old cliché, "the devil you know is better than the devil you don't" applies here. What might our church become if newcomers arrive with different ideas about what the church ought to be? New ideas, new faces, new questions: these can all be quite threatening to the status quo. When the church is in the business of maintaining the institution, newcomers can be a threat. However, when the church has a vision for disciple-making and Christian transformation, a basic commitment to evangelism and outreach is essential. Welcoming newcomers is not only a good idea, but it is imperative if the church is to remain true to its calling. For many churches, this is a monumental shift in perspective. To grow is to change, and to change can be emotionally devastating. Our commitment to reaching new people has an impact not only on their lives, but on the lives and faith development of existing church members. Therefore, the ministries of outreach intrinsically affect the strengthening and nurturing ministries of the existing congregation. Long-time members and participants in the congregation need to be both "instructed" and "cared" into an outreach perspective. As a manifestation of the stewardship of the church, both newcomers and incumbents need to be equally appreciated and nurtured. The management of this delicate balance is truly an art. The long-term health of a congregation depends on it.

Reaching out into the community does more than serve the needs of the church. Reaching out is an act of servanthood to Christ and the world. Stewards are servants. The needs or desires of the servant are sublimated to the needs of the one being served. In John 13, Jesus washed the disciples' feet and told them that was their work from that time forward. As Christ became a servant, so must all disciples accept a life of service to others. Paul instructed the church at Philippi to emulate the *kenosis*, the self-emptying, of Jesus Christ (Philippians 2:3-11). A great learning of stewardship has to do with what it means to be a servant. In fact, servanthood—putting faith into action—is a basic piece in the definition of Christian stewardship. This commitment to servanthood illustrates how the primary task of the church is not linear, but cyclical—moving along an ever-heightening spiral. Before we can serve, we learn servanthood by being related to the mission and ministry of Jesus Christ and by being instructed in this work. Then we are strengthened and nurtured in our commitment; afterward, we are sent forth to put into practice what we have learned. Put another way: We are called to serve. As we serve, we find the need for support and strength. We return to the fellowship of believers for growth and development. As we grow and find our strength, we desire once more to put our faith into practice—and so it goes. Christian stewards are perpetually reaching out to receive and serve in the name of Jesus Christ.

Stewards Relate People to God

Melanie C., a twenty-something secretary from Tennessee, explains why she transferred her membership to a new church: "I belonged to my last church for seven years. When friends asked me to come along to a Bible study at their church, I gave all kinds of excuses, but finally caved in. We were studying the Letter to the Romans. I went home from that ninety-minute study with my head spinning. I learned more about the Bible in those ninety minutes than I had learned in the past seven years at my own church. Why go to church if you don't understand God any better than if you stayed home? That's why I switched churches."

The role of the church as steward of the gospel of Jesus Christ cannot be overemphasized. The church is in a unique position to educate people about the Bible and to help them relate better to Jesus Christ. As Melanie C. points out, "If I'm not going to get it (understanding about God, Christ, the Bible, and so forth) at church, where am I going to get it?" The church exercises faithful stewardship to the degree that it connects people to Christ and facilitates clear understanding.

This challenges the traditional notion that Christian stewardship is concerned with the individual believer's use of time, talent, and resources. Not that time, talent, and resources are not central to Christian stewardship, but the focus is broader than these things. Stewardship cannot occur apart from discipleship. And discipleship—that process of relating people to God and to one another—cannot occur apart from an understanding of the spiritual gifts operative within the Christian community. The church's task of making disciples extends to enable people to discover, understand, and develop their gifts as well as deploy them. So often, individuals are asked to give, without having a clear understanding of *what* they have to give. As we help people relate to God in Jesus Christ, we also help them to discover the gifts that God has given them. People tend to relate better to others who are already attempting to relate to them. Helping seekers after Christ to see that God has already been bestowing gifts upon them creates an avenue for making connections.

Before we can give, we must first receive. The church often places heavy emphasis upon giving, but it is less intentional about receiving. The apostle Paul states that God "loves a cheerful giver" (2 Corinthians 9:7). That cheer, that sense of joy, comes from a deep appreciation of God's beneficence. So often, the spiritual development of the believer is stunted by demands for responses that he or she is not ready to give. The church may place expectations upon the believer that exceed where he or she is along the faith journey. When churches take the time to help believers discover their giftedness, they reap a much greater bounty in the long run. It is simpler to give from abundance than from scarcity. When people believe that they are gifted and blessed, they are more likely to be joyful. When people are joyful, they are more likely to be liberal and generous givers of all they have.

Steven L., a pastor in Minnesota, tells of a woman who attended a spiritual gifts discovery workshop and came home a transformed person. "Lydia returned to the church all excited because her primary gifts were compassion and giving. She told everyone that she had always cared about other people, but had never done anything with her caring. When she came to see her concern as a gift, she was motivated to put her faith into action. She's a fireball! She has single-handedly started three new outreach programs into the community and has organized several people in the church to help her. Before, she only came to church on Sundays; now, if she's not at church every day, people worry about her." This kind of energy and excitement is generated when the church takes seriously the opportunity to help seekers discover and develop their gifts and resources for ministry. Much more will be said concerning spiritual gifts in Chapter 4.

Spiritual gifts programs illustrate one significant shift in the way church leaders relate to members in a congregation. Spiritual gifts discovery tools are a way of listening to the people in our churches. Instead of the church telling people what they should do and on what committee they should serve, a process of mutual discovery occurs. The more deeply we listen to the people in our churches, and the more helpful we are in enabling them to learn more about themselves and their relationship to God, the better able we are to understand their passions. When people are passionate about something, they commit themselves completely to whatever it is that matters most. The object of our deepest caring and concern motivates us to give our time, energy, money, ability, and best effort. When leaders in the church effectively connect people's passions to the mission and ministry of the congregation, amazing things can occur.

The church's function, then, of relating believers to God through Christ Jesus is a two-way process. Not only does the church teach ways to move believers closer to Christ, but it also removes the obstacles that make it difficult to see all the ways that God is already reaching out to us. We discover what we have to give as we discern all that God has placed at our disposal. This is a vital stewardship function of the second aspect of the church's primary task, namely, relating believers to Jesus Christ. As we continue to enable believers to relate to God in new ways, we also work to strengthen and nurture them in that relationship; and we offer new ways to put their gifts of time, talent, and resources to good use.

Stewards Strengthen and Nurture Believers in Their Faith

James J., a retired research and development manager for Bell Labs, remarks: "My church has a clear understanding that I should be a good steward, but it has no concept of its own stewardship. I spent my life learning how to manage materials to create new things, but I also had to learn to manage people in order to get things done. Managing material resources is only one side of the equation; managing people is the other. My church looks at the materials we have to manage, but it doesn't look at the people."

The parable of the talents in Matthew 25:14-30 illustrates that faithful stewardship requires wise investment. Wise investment requires a two-tiered view of reality that takes into consideration both the short term and the long term. We spend in the present; we invest toward the future. We are quite adept at spending in the short term, but not so proficient at investing for the long term. The church has a responsibility to manage both the short-term and the long-term mission of the church. The time and effort that are invested in strengthening and nurturing the Christian fellowship yield long-term benefits. Unfortunately, so many churches focus on short-term, immediate needs that long-term investment gets lost. This is especially true of the financial stewardship needs of our congregations, where the short-term financial crises that we face prevent us from addressing the long-term funding processes that could strengthen and revitalize our churches.

Strengthening and nurturing believers in the faith can be viewed as a coaching/training function in the church. A number of years ago, a baseball player named Dan Driessen played for the Cincinnati Reds. Very quickly Driessen was tagged far and wide as a young man with "great natural ability." He appeared on the scene already a gifted ballplayer, but he was not great. All the talk of natural ability prevented Driessen from improving for a long time. It was not until the coaches and trainers began working with him that his talent really blossomed and he showed phenomenal improvement. Taking the raw materials that Driessen came with, coaches were able to elevate him to the next level. Similarly, a crucial stewardship function of the church is to strengthen and nurture believers in the Christian faith: to serve as the coach/mentor that can elevate disciples-in-formation to the next level of faith development.

Just as spiritual gifts discovery is an important ministry in the church, so are the ways in which we help believers develop their talents and grow in their faith. Children learn and grow in a safe, nurturing, and caring environment. The same is true of evolving Christians. The church serves its participants well when it provides new opportunities to put faith into action. The organizational structure that we adopt in our churches may very well enhance or impede our faithful stewardship of the people, talents, and resources at our disposal. The process of nominations, often viewed as a nuisance by many, can be a valuable system for connecting believers to the mission and ministry of Jesus Christ.

The pastor is the chairperson of the nominations committee in The United Methodist Church. He or she occupies a unique position within the church. One role of the pastor in the stewardship of the congregation is to act as a "terminal" where connections are made between the mission and vision of the fellowship and the giftedness of the men and women who serve the church. Even in the largest church, the pastor plays a crucial role of facilitating the empowerment and deployment of laity for ministry. Unless the pastor understands the importance of this role, poor stewardship may result. The church might not fully use the resources and gifts that God has placed within it.

Strengthening and nurturing the faith is a complex process. At times, the two processes of strengthening and nurturing are at odds with each other. Many of the situations that strengthen faith are challenging, difficult, and even threatening. Family crises, the loss of loved ones, loss of a job, dealing with addictions, or broken relationships all test and can strengthen our faith, but we do not feel nurtured by these experiences. One way to view these experiences is to compare them to muscle building. The process of building muscle is violent. Tissue is torn and destroyed, but the hardened scar cells that replace it are, in fact, the muscle. Muscle building is a continual process of tearing and healing. After a strenuous workout, nothing feels better than a massage or a trip to the whirlpool. The workout is necessary, and its benefit depends on how strenuous it is; but it can be followed by something very nurturing and pleasurable. In fact, unless there is something pleasurable about the experience, it will be very difficult to maintain the discipline necessary to succeed. While "no pain, no gain" is the motivational motto of a lot of athletes, it might read more truthfully, "All pain, no gain."

The church needs to steer clear of the thinking that "real" faith lies at one extreme or the other. Some churches give the impression that the church is not the place for pleasure. "We are committed to the Lord's work," they seem to say, "and that is serious business. We aren't in this for fun, but because it's the right thing to do." Joy is absent, and every experience within the congregation is "for its own good." One of my friends calls these congregations "cod liver oil churches." The other extreme he calls "warm fuzzy fellowships," because the focus is on making the members feel good. Nurture of the membership is the priority. The church where I grew up had no sense of itself in the community or the world. One of the pastors said of this church that it was "a haven, a port in the storm, a safe place where the rest of the world could be shut out." Those words still haunt me. While that fellowship was very caring to one another, it was dead to any greater purpose. Strengthening and nurturing a congregation is a balancing act; the two processes become one process. There is always an appropriate tension between the two to keep the church healthy and growing, but even these are not enough. Believers are strengthened and nurtured for a purpose—to take their faith out into the world.

Stewards Are Sent Out Into the World

Chad W. gives twenty hours a week to volunteer work in addition to his full-time job. He has made it a priority to serve the needs of his community through his church, but it has not been easy. Chad reflects: "I used to get so mad at my church. We have been in this neighborhood for over 150 years. We have 725 members, and we have an annual budget of over one million dollars. We have an endowment fund of 2.5 million. We are three blocks from some of the highest priced homes and condos on one side, and five blocks from some of the most horrible slum housing you've ever seen. Three years ago, Price Wesleyan Church got a new pastor who had a vision for serving the community. Now, Price has about 75 members with a $50,000 budget. You should have seen the ministry they created! A soup kitchen, a thrift shop, an after school program, an abuse counseling program, a literacy program, a 'Help for the Homeless' council, and an assistance program for single mothers all got started within a year. My church was doing nothing! We had the people, we had the resources, we had the facility; but they had the vision. They exercised the stewardship. It made me sick to see another church *doing* what we only talked about."

It cannot be stated too emphatically: the stewardship of the church depends upon putting faith into action; carrying the gospel from the church out into the world. Unless a church is participating in all four aspects of its primary task, it is not modeling good stewardship. The institutional church is a means to an end; that end is the church universal, the body of Christ. When a local congregation grows satisfied existing as an end in itself, it begins to die. Chad W. saw that his church should not be satisfied with mere existence. That is why he mobilized his church for action. Chad saw the work of the sister Wesleyan church as a challenge to move. Single-handedly, he recruited volunteers to participate in a variety of ministries in the community. Chad encouraged his pastor to go with him to talk to the Wesleyan pastor to offer support for the work of the Wesleyan church. Chad presented a vision to the congregation. Even more, Chad presented himself to drive and direct that vision. His pastor, Carol, says of Chad, "I have never, never encountered anyone who was more willing to put his money and time and energy where his mouth is than Chad. He is every pastor's dream of a committed layperson. I think how much we are doing with one Chad. Just think what I could do with two or three!"

That is the stewardship role of the church: to empower and enable "Chads." Our primary task, the way we fulfill our mission, is to reach out and receive people, to relate them to Christ and the church, to strengthen and nurture them in their faith, and to send them out to serve in the name and power of Jesus Christ. If there are not enough Chads in the church, it may well be that the church is not fulfilling its primary task. When stewardship is limited to the annual financial commitment campaign to fund the budget of the local church, our opportunity to create visionary Christian stewards is severely limited, if not altogether impossible. A new vision for stewardship—as caretakers of the church's primary task, mission, and purpose—is needed.

Conclusion

Just as the earth is not a fixed entity at the center of the universe, so the church is not a fixed entity at the center of creation. The church that is fixed is the church that is dead. Christ's church is alive, dynamic, expanding, progressive, and improving. Christ's followers are alive, striving, learning, growing, and serving. As the church, we revolve around the Source of all light and life. God provides the energy, the Spirit, and the orbit that we follow. Copernicus presented the solar system as an alternative to the geocentered (earth-centered) theory that no longer adequately explained reality. Perhaps we need to dislodge the church from the center of our reality so that God might rightfully resume that position. Maybe then the church will begin to *move* once more.

Questions for Reflection and Discussion

1. How does our church participate in the four aspects of our primary task? In which of the four aspects are we the strongest? the weakest?

2. What is our vision for our church? How does the primary task affect our vision?

3. In what ways has our church become stationary? What traditions and practices keep us from moving?

4. What is our definition of stewardship? How do we communicate our definition? How does the discussion of stewardship in light of the primary task affect our definition?

5. How does our church appreciate and manage the resources and opportunities for ministry that God has given us? How can we improve these processes of appreciation and management?

CHAPTER 2

What is flat, has four corners, and demons all around?
"We have always done it this way"

 map of the sixteenth century depicts the "known world" as a Euro-centered land mass surrounded by water. Brown barren outlying lands stand in vivid contrast to the lush land of Italy and Gaul. The waters darken as they stretch toward the edges. At the farthest reaches, serpents, gargoyles, behemoths, and leviathans patrol ominously. The four compass points are bisected by pointers to the "four corners" of the earth. Each corner is host to an elemental: air, water, fire, and earth. These elementals guard the fate of all who dwell upon the face of the earth. They have been sent by God to sustain life. No mortal may look upon the visage of an elemental. No mortal will survive an encounter with a beast that dwells beyond the known world. In the lower right hand corner of the map is an inscription: "the heavenly vantage."

This was the map that graced the table of Nicolaus Copernicus. For centuries, debate had endured over the shape, the size, and the dimensions of the earth. The church argued about whether the earth was finite or infinite; ending beyond the oceans or stretching forever onward into eternity. Arguing into yet another century, astronomers finally concluded that the earth might in fact be a sphere, consistent with all other known planets and stars. The church rejected this theory. Copernicus seriously considered the testimony of sailors who reported a curvature to the horizon. He noted frequently in his journal that the earth might not be flat at all. Galileo furthered the theories of Copernicus, but once again was forced by the church to renounce such thinking.

The church of the sixteenth and seventeenth centuries resisted the picture of the earth as a sphere drifting in space because of references to the four corners of the earth in the Bible. The church used the books of Ezekiel and Revelation to defend the "flat earth" hypothesis. In fact, it defended the "flat earth" even more intensely than it did the centrality of the earth to the universe. For the church, the integrity and infallibility of the Bible were at stake. The official Vatican acknowledgment of the spherical shape of our planet did not come until the NASA Saturn missions in the late 1950's and the early 1960's.

Contemporary churches often suffer a "flat earth" mentality. Denominations work hard to define their doctrine and polity. The forms, rituals, and structures of a church take decades, even centuries, to form. Using their own traditions and practices, local churches build upon the formal framework of their denominational connections. An informal "book of practices" gets written in the hearts and minds of the members of the church. These tacit understandings of the local church are etched in stone as deeply and lastingly as the Ten Commandments were carved into the Sinai tablets.

These traditions and practices are a valuable part of the life of the church. They help shape the identity of each particular fellowship. Leaders within our congregations are to function as stewards of these identifying customs. Good stewardship means drawing life and strength from these customs, rather than allowing them to place the church in bondage. So many new and innovative ideas are dispatched to the outer darkness by the familiar words: "We have never done it that way before."

The problem with maps is that they do more than chart a course; they also shape a reality. Once we become familiar with the manner in which a map defines an area, it is nearly impossible to see it in any other way. How true this is in the church. Once we see the "right" way to do things in the church, we find it hard to see other "right" ways that might emerge.

A key stewardship function of a church's leadership is to question the existing maps, to continually seek to gain "the heavenly vantage," and to serve the cartographic role of creating new maps. In this chapter, we see what happens when churches become bound by the "we-have-always-done-it-this-way" mentality. By addressing the fact that many of our maps are out of date, we can begin to chart new maps that better define the territory of the twenty-first century frontier. ■

How do we define Christian stewardship? How do we determine what kinds of ministries and practices we should engage in through the church? Who settles disputes? Who is responsible for decisions? What is our authority?

Every church has a "handbook." Actually, there are at least two handbooks. One of them (we hope) is the Bible. The other handbook is the set of rules and regulations that helps define the churches in each denomination or communion. Most denominations have written guidelines, disciplines, or bylaws. These documents make up the formal side of the handbook. The informal side of the handbook is the way each congregation interprets and lives out its understanding of the doctrine and polity of the denomination. When it wants to answer the questions posed at the beginning of this section, each church refers to its handbook.

Stewardship in the church is the process of appreciating and managing the resources and opportunities for ministry that God gives us. It is constantly striving to live up to our full potential from God's perspective, rather than from a more limited human perspective. Polity and doctrine facilitate the practice of managing our resources and ministries. Interpreted rightly, these tenets provide a sound foundation upon which to build the church. However, doctrine easily devolves into dogma; consequently, the cornerstone of our foundation can become a millstone around the neck. The doctrine of the church quickly becomes that which informs us of what we *may not* do instead of helping us to understand what we *may* do.

A young pastor (asking to remain *completely* anonymous) talks of her experience in her first appointment. Her story is important for any church leader who would be a faithful steward of the mission, core process, and purpose of the church.

"The very first week of my appointment, the trustees, the administrative board, the finance committee, and the council on ministries were to meet on four successive nights. At first, I thought they were doing this for my benefit. I soon found out differently. The second week, the pastor-parish relations, Christian education, and missions committees met. Each meeting was scheduled from 7:00 P.M. to 10:30 P.M.! Remember, this is a church of only eighty-five members. The average age of the members in the church was probably sixty. When I arrived at the first meeting, the chairperson gave me a copy of *Robert's Rules of Order*. We had a three-page agenda. It was unreal. The trustees had a chairperson, a vice chairperson, a secretary, a parliamentarian, a *Book of Discipline* interpreter, a timekeeper, a treasurer, and a historian who had a copy of every set of minutes of the board of trustees since 1963. All I could think of was 'Candid Camera.' I mean, I kept waiting for Allen Funt to step out of the closet to tell me it was a joke. I sat with my mouth gaping open for three-and-a-half hours. It was awful.

"The next three nights were more of the same. Each committee took as much time looking up things in the minutes, the *Discipline*, and *Robert's Rules of Order* as it did actually accomplishing anything. After two months, I stopped sleeping and I started to get an ulcer. I finally made a decision. I arrived at the administrative board meeting one night with my copy of *Robert's Rules of Order*, the *Book of Discipline*, our church committee roster of officers, a bucket, some lighter fluid, and a book of matches. I doused the books and papers, set them afire, and told the leaders of the church that we were going back to zero. No *Book of Discipline*, no *Robert's Rules of Order*, no charge conference elections, nothing.

"I still remember the looks on the faces of the people in that room. They were convinced that I had lost my mind. Maybe I did lose my mind, or maybe I found it. I sat down and asked the question, 'What are we going to do now?' The first answer I got was that we would get another *Book of Discipline* and *Robert's Rules of Order*. I stood my ground. I challenged the chairperson of the board to describe the church in terms other than our 'official' procedures. Anyway, as the meeting progressed, we began to catch a vision for the church that wasn't defined for us by a book. People began to share their frustration that our meetings were torture; that we never seemed to get anything done. Three people talked about how tired they were. One woman served on six committees, and she enjoyed none of them. When we left the church that evening, everyone was in agreement about just one thing: what we had been doing wasn't working, and we wanted to figure out something new."

The church that this young pastor serves is growing and healthy. It developed a new structure, and it is organized almost exclusively in small-group committees and project teams. There is more joy and energy in the church than had been experienced in years. No one has carried a copy of *Robert's Rules of Order* to a meeting in more than a year. And what of the *Book of Discipline*?

The pastor relates: "Of course we use the *Discipline*. My point was never to do away with the *Book of Discipline*; it's indispensable. It's just that my church was being slowly killed by law. It needed a shot of grace to save it. No longer does our church exist to serve the *Discipline*; the *Discipline* exists to serve the church. It's great to get things straight. It was like we were trying to navigate a brand new place with a thirty-year-old map."

Maps again. This story illustrates how difficult it is to get anywhere today with old, outdated charts and graphs. This pastor's story raises three important issues: the need to know who we are before we try to do ministry; the need to evaluate our processes; and the need for permission to be creative in our church settings.

This small church originally structured itself to be *organized*, not to be *effective*. It was so focused on doing things right that it lost sight of doing the right things. It answered the question of how to do its work before it understood the work it was supposed to do. It structured itself as a much larger church than it really was, and its unwieldy form threatened to collapse under its own weight. There are three fundamental stewardship questions that each fellowship should wrestle with: who are we, whose are we, and what are we doing here? These are the questions that we would do well to ask and answer before we put our organizational and procedural systems in place.

The lay leaders of this small church surprised one another when they shared their common assessment that the current structure was not working. Though everyone knew that things were not working well, no one could identify why. New programs were tried, new committees were formed, and more responsibilities were created. In assessing the problems within the church, the focus was on what the church did, not on how the church operated. The church leadership determined to work harder, not smarter. The harder they worked, the more tired everyone became. A new pastor brought a new perspective. Instead of looking at the programs of the church, she forced everyone to examine the systems for ministry. She challenged the congregation to examine their sense of mission and purpose, their core values, and their structures and processes for leadership. Almost immediately, good things began to happen.

While the old adage claims that "nothing succeeds like success," the pastor I spoke with was very nervous that she would be in trouble should the conference leadership ever find out about the "book burning" incident. She claims that she "doctored" her charge conference records the previous year to comply with all the requirements. It is unfortunate that someone who is so creative in her own local church has to toe the line when it comes to the unexamined processes within the larger church. Fear of sanctions forced this pastor, as she put it, "to be sure to color inside the lines."

Stewardship requires faithful appreciation and management at denominational levels just as it does at the local church level. If our organizational policies are debilitating influences, it becomes imperative for our denominational leaders to provide permission for pushing the limits of the existing system. In The United Methodist Church, the *Book of Discipline* suggests many different structures for ministry, but it *requires* very few. While it offers guidelines for organizing administrative structures, the *Discipline* allows for a wide variety of different manifestations. Sadly, the *Book of Discipline* is often used to set limits and boundaries instead of to open new possibilities.[6] We need good stewards at all levels of church leadership to empower our congregations to thrive under grace, rather than perish under law. Denominational leaders promote growth and strength when they extend permission to local congregations to do what is necessary to structure themselves for effective and vital ministry.

One of the areas that greatly needs an infusion of grace in the local church is the domain of financial stewardship. It seems that finance committees are especially prone to legalism and to perpetuating time-worn practices. These practices become deep ruts that most churches never even identify as problems. Because they have had a measure of success at some time in the life of the church, these practices are heralded as sacred in the present. They become the institutionalized paradigms for our behavior. Instead of freeing us to be creative and effective, these practices limit us, and they create boundaries that impede and restrict us. In fact, they make us less successful than we might otherwise be. Three such practices are: the annual funding campaign, the budgeting process, and the narrow definition of stewardship in the church that equates stewardship with money.

The Annual Funding Campaign

Ask almost any long-time church member about his or her first memory of an annual stewardship campaign in the church, and he or she will answer, "the mid-1950's." The earliest financial stewardship campaign that I have been able to locate is Samuel Walter's *Year of Tithing*, published in 1956. Prior to this time, giving campaigns were called just that: they were not given the qualifier "stewardship." More broad-based visitation/canvassing campaigns existed from the 1930's and 1940's, but the purely financial stewardship campaign apparently emerged later. During the 1960's, very few of these campaigns were published. It was early in the 1970's, in the wake of the OPEC embargo, runaway inflation, and decreasing church membership, that funding campaigns began to proliferate. What once existed as a rare curiosity quickly became standard practice. Early accounts reported exceptional responses to financial stewardship campaigns. They were new, they were unique, and they opened for discussion a topic that had rarely been addressed—giving.

Giving to God through the church has long been a subject of preaching, but the amount given was a matter between the believer and God. The reason for this is simple: until the 1970's, the majority of churches in North America received all the money they needed without having to ask for it. Giving was a normal part of church participation. During the late 1940's through the early 1960's, church participation increased. As more people came to church, bringing their wallets and purses, the coffers bulged. Money was available for missions. Money was available for education. Money was available to expand church facilities to include gymnasiums, parlors, and state-of-the-art kitchens and offices. There was no practical motivation to ask for more.

The 1970's brought monumental changes to the church. The combination of fewer people and higher costs began to pinch the church severely. Outgo surpassed income. Bills mounted, deficits occurred for the first time ever, and church leaders found themselves in the awkward position of having to "remind" people to give to the church. The vast majority of church members had spent their entire lives supporting a church with no mention of money unless there was a specific need. The most common reaction to "money talk" in the church was that it was not spiritual and not appropriate.

Giving, long a subject of Christian stewardship, suddenly became a hot topic. Previously, giving was viewed as an important practice in the development of faithful Christian disciples. With the financial crisis erupting in the seventies, the benefits of giving shifted from the *giver* to the *church as institution*. The problems associated with such a shift will be explored in Chapter 4, but the response to this shift was to institute the "fall campaign" as the new orthodoxy for funding the mission and ministry of the church.

At their very best, annual funding campaigns can teach participants in local congregations that their giving is an essential part of their faith formation and growth as Christian disciples. A well-conceived, well-run financial stewardship campaign has the power to boost members to the next level of commitment in their life of faith. When Christian stewardship is taught as a key component of the faith journey, it carries with it the transforming power of the Holy Spirit. At their worst, financial stewardship campaigns are a stop-gap solution to a fundamental problem. They can work wonders to underwrite a single year's budget, but it is questionable whether they actually do anything to change people's long-term giving habits. True stewardship is a growth process that requires continuous learning and improvement. Most financial stewardship campaigns are designed to meet short-term commitments, not alter long-term behavior.

In addition, churches that have used funding campaigns for a number of years report a "law of diminishing returns" effect. The law of diminishing returns states that the more of something you are exposed to, the less satisfaction you receive. That first bite of cheese-cake might be heaven; but by the last bite, your senses have dulled to its powerful effect. A second piece might still taste fine; but before long, desire turns to satiation, then to revulsion. Hence the saying, "too much of a good thing." The most dangerous thing about stewardship campaigns is that they work, and often work well. An addiction builds with each passing year.

Addiction is a fitting illustration. A funding campaign is run, and the results address the crisis, but not the root problem. Time passes. Another crisis arises. Another campaign is sought. It brings relief. The next year, more money is needed, and a better program is devised. Each program requires more work to top the goal set the year before. As the novelty of the programs begins to wear thin, people become less influenced by each new incarnation. More work yields fewer results. The search for the perfect program brings frustration. Before long, the church finds itself trapped in a downward spiral.

Granted, not all churches experience these kinds of problems. There are many churches that run annual funding campaigns, and they thrive upon them. However, they are the exceptions, not the rule. Most annual campaigns are designed to address the immediate and short-term financial needs of the institution; they are not designed to be a teaching tool for the transformational growth of Christians. Nothing is inherently wrong with funding campaigns. The problem seems to be their application.

Historically, this is a case where temporary measures became institutionalized as standard operating procedure. Annual funding campaigns were never intended to replace a fundamental understanding of and commitment to financial giving by Christian disciples. Campaigns were intended to be one means among many to help educate people about the important place of sacrificial giving in the life of faith. Churches found that annual funding campaigns delivered fine results when they were first employed, so they soon became regular practice, replacing ongoing, integrated stewardship education. Another such practice that found a home in The United Methodist Church is a pesky critter known as the unified budget.

Budgeting in the Church

Following the second World War, the United States went through a unifying frenzy. We developed the United Nations, the United Way, and the National Council of Churches. Corporate America designed a new way of budgeting and labeled it "unified budgeting." The premise was simple. Auditing and regulating the finances of an institution could be greatly simplified by placing all sources of income and all expenses under one single budget with different categories. Rather than individual budgets for different departments or offices, everything would be handled from a central location. The unified budget became the budget of preference in business in 1948, and the budget of preference in The United Methodist Church by 1952. In 1956, corporate America realized that unified budgets were a dismal failure, and they stopped using them. As of 1996, the unified budget is still the budget of choice in most churches.

Why has it taken the church four decades to realize something that the business world learned in just eight short years? There are actually some sensible reasons. Unified budgets make record keeping easier; and since many churches use the services of nonprofessional volunteers to do their record keeping, this makes sense. There is much less work involved in developing a unified budget, so less is required of volunteer finance committees. Additionally, unified budgets work very smoothly when income consistently covers all expenses, which was the reality of most churches from the late-1940's through the early- to mid-1970's. However, the landscape has been changing constantly in the past few decades, and the budgeting maps are in serious need of updating.

Most people give to the things that matter most to them. Givers are more inclined to give to programs and people than to budgets. In a culture where there is so much competition for charitable dollars, the agency or organization that can make the most enticing appeal is likely to receive the largest gifts. No matter how well a person loves his or her church, he or she still wants to be assured that the money given makes a difference. Giving a "fair share" to keep a church functioning does not touch the heart and faith nearly so effectively as giving to save a life, or to help someone in need, or to provide an education for a child. Budgets are a tool of the church to help plan for the ministry needs of the church, but they do very little to actually communicate those needs. So often, the budget becomes an end in itself, and it communicates nothing more than the church's short-term fiscal picture.

Very few people know how to read and make sense of a line-item budget. Putting the facts and figures in black and white may not be getting the message across. Just because every member of a church receives a copy of the annual budget does not guarantee that anyone will know what the church is doing with the money it receives. Many funds that are apportioned by the annual conference in The United

Methodist Church have a label that tells very little about how the funds are used. When a church member sees a budget amount designated for Church World Service, what does he or she really know about that line-item? The little used designation of "Disciplinary Obligations" offers almost no explanation about what this money is used to accomplish. There is absolutely no connection between the potential ministry to be served and the heart-motivated desire to give. If the church hopes to engage people in missional outreach, it may need to provide a lot more information. Even beyond information, the church needs to answer the parishioner's question, "Why should I care?"

Unified budgets do not illuminate, but instead conceal the work of the church. Different people give to different needs for different reasons. Some people care deeply about the educational needs of the local congregation; others pride themselves on the support that they provide to the pastoral staff; while still others give liberally to mission work at home and abroad. Some people are committed to the care and maintenance of the church facilities; others to supporting the fellowship programs of the church; and yet others to making sure that the youth group has its material needs cared for. Unified budgets inhibit a sense of supporting the things that mean the most to individuals within the fellowship.

There are many alternatives to unified budgets. Designated budgets, term budgets, and project budgets are just a few. Actually, these are not exclusive of one another. Most churches that claim to use a unified budget still have "pockets" of designated giving within the church. Most United Methodist Women's (UMW) fellowships, United Methodist Youth Fellowships (UMYF), and United Methodist Men's (UMM) groups have their own budgets and treasuries. Many church school classes have their own funds. Often, endowed funds and the interest that they generate are handled separately by the board of trustees. We fool ourselves when we think that we ever fully adopted a unified budget approach. However, we can learn some valuable lessons from the designated budgets within our congregations.

First, when small groups have their own treasuries, there is usually a clearer sense of where the money comes from, where it goes, and what benefit is received. Requests are more specific, and a greater number of people understand what is needed and why. Second, more people take ownership of projects and ministries. When a group with a clear identity commits to making something happen, more people take responsibility for the project or process. Frances G., a UMW chairperson, says: "I give more money to the UMW than I do to the church. The only time I ever hear about money in the church is when there isn't enough. No one ever lets me know what my money accomplishes. But here, in the women's group, I can see exactly where my money gets spent, and I'm proud of it. I want to give more because I know it will do some good." It is important to people to know that the gift they give has meaning. Giving cements believers into the Christian body. People want their gifts to matter.

Active participants in the church understand that there are some basic financial needs of the institution and that not all giving can or should be designated. Yet when we constantly find ourselves falling short of our financial goals, we should analyze both our methods and our motivations for seeking funds. Individuals will give only so much from a sense of duty or obligation. Herb M., from Pittsburgh, offers this understanding: "I *know* that I need to support my church, but I *want* to do something special. You can explain to me what needs to be done, and I will give a certain amount to support that. But if you can show me something special, something that I care about personally, then I will probably come up with a whole lot more. I'll give something because I know I ought to, but I will give more if you give me a reason to really want to." So much of what passes for financial stewardship appeals mainly to our "head" processes rather than to our "heart" processes. Herb M.'s comments indicate that the two are not the same thing. When we move beyond the "good reasons" for giving to those that touch the hearts of individual believers, we open a whole new vista for giving and commitment.

However, merely designating funds is not enough. Barbara S., a Presbyterian from New Jersey, laments: "We were given a sizable gift designated for handbells for a handbell choir to be formed. We will probably never have a handbell choir, so the money just sits, year after year, doing absolutely no good for anyone." Designated budgets that are too narrowly defined are not practical. Designated categories need to be specific enough to appeal to people's interests, but general enough for the church to have some flexibility in using them. Also, the *church* defines the categories of designation, not the giver. When givers try to control too tightly how their gifts should be used, they are binding a church's ability to function. A valuable lesson for the church is that it is completely proper to refuse to accept a gift. There are countless stories of gifts of property made to churches that were unable to dispose of these gifts and that ended up saddled with great expense for maintaining the property over the years. One Tennessee church had a Memorial Gifts Account with a balance in excess of $100,000 that was virtually unspendable because of the specificity of the givers' designations. People need to understand how to give, and it is the responsibility of the church to teach giving. To help a giver understand why a gift is not appropriate or why the church cannot accept it is as important as encouraging a giver to make a commitment in the first place. Some may be offended when their gifts are not taken, but more often a compromise can be worked out that pleases the giver and that truly benefits the church.

For a designated budget to provide advantages over a unified budget, clear and precise communication must occur. If the budgets of specific committees are to be designated accounts, separate from the general budget, the appropriate committees can provide a valuable service to the church by creating clear, concise money usage policies. Giving to both designated and undesignated budget accounts is facilitated by well-articulated money usage/spending plans. Often, great strife occurs in a congregation when undesignated money is received, and the church attempts to figure out what to do with it. If a money usage policy is already in place, then both designated and undesignated gifts are true windfalls to the congregation.

Two other popular budgeting practices are term and project budgets. A term budget is a budget that covers a specific span of time. Most churches create annual budgets that follow the calendar year. However, a great number of churches have discovered that one year is too short a time frame in which to do adequate planning. Since the ministries of the church are ongoing and many develop over a long period of time, budgets are developed to cover a span of two, three, five, or more years. Steve S. of Indiana reports that in his church a three-year term budget "blew the roof off giving! When we talked three years, we dreamed really big dreams and people got excited. We got very specific about what we wanted money for. We developed four or five different ways for people to make commitments and give, and more people responded than ever before. By thinking in longer terms, we actually did a better job than when we were limited by a year-to-year process."

Many people are less bothered by a three-year $500,000 budget than they are by a budget of $150,000 per year. Even though the first amount is higher than the total for all three years of the second budget, for some reason people accept it as more reasonable. Psychologically, a longer time frame allows people to move beyond a "maintenance mentality" within the church to see possibilities for growth and mission. Detractors will comment that it is impossible to know what the needs will be three years down the road. However, the same can be said of the needs three months down the road. The history of the Christian faith encourages us to push the limits and to strive forward into mystery and the unknown. This "stepping out in faith" is a fundamental characteristic of the Christian church. Anything that invites us to move beyond our limitations to realize our full potential is to be welcomed.

Project budgets also help us look at what we can do, rather than what we cannot do. Regardless of the time frame, a project budget looks at a program, a ministry, or an event and simply asks, "What will it cost?" A budget is then created that will fund the need. How many times has a new idea or proposal died at the committee table when someone issued the verdict, "We can't do it—we didn't budget for it!" Money should not be the primary reason for deciding whether or not to do something in the church. If there is a need for a mission or ministry, the money should be found. There is absolutely no rule that a new project cannot create its own budget. Allowing the budget to "drive" what is possible in the church is a practice that needs to be changed.

Many capital funds campaigns fall into term- and project-budget categories. They are designated, clearly communicated, and often highly successful. They tend to speak to people's hearts and souls as well as to their heads. We can learn some useful lessons from capital campaigns for the ongoing funding needs in the church.

The type of budget a church uses ought to fit the administrative needs and the unique personality of the congregation. Some churches are doing well with a unified budget. Many small churches labor under the unified budget process. Alternative budgeting is not difficult, but it requires some serious thought and planning. There is no guarantee that adopting a new budgeting process will make much difference, especially if communication does not improve. Peter B., a retired pastor in Delaware, states: "You can design the finest, most professional, most appropriate budget in the world and people still won't support it if they don't understand it. Unified budgets are not the problem. The problem is that we don't help people interpret the budget we've got. Conferences don't help churches know where the money goes. Pastors don't help congregations know where the money goes. Finance committees don't help governing boards know where the money goes. It's all communication."

While the problem may not *all* be communication, certainly communication is a substantial part of it. Since line-item budgets and bottom-line figures do not communicate to the vast majority of our congregations, it would be good for us to seek alternative means of communication. Whether a unified, designated, project, term, or other form of budget is used, it might be helpful to present it as a *narrative budget*.[7] A narrative budget tells the story of what happens to the giver's dollar after it lands in the plate. It puts faces and names and projects to the requests for funds. It connects the giver to the need, and it engages him or her in the mission and ministry of the church. A narrative budget allows the individual to understand how his or her gift makes a difference. It provides a context that is missing from line-item budgets.

The narrative budget also provides a reference point. The pastor and other leaders of the church can refer to the narrative budget to bring people status reports and to move toward future askings. It puts in print the dreams and possibilities for ministry, and it enables people to talk about the work of the church based on a common understanding. Joyce K., a local pastor in Vermont, began using a narrative budget in 1992, after expressing serious doubts that it would have much impact. In 1995, Joyce reported: "I won't go so far as to say that it's a miracle or anything, but it has been unbelievable to see the difference it has made. Our giving is the best it's been in years, which actually isn't saying much; but at this rate, we will be able to pay our apportionments in full and meet our budget in full within the next couple of years. In three years, we have seen a fifteen percent increase in giving each year, from $48,000 to $73,000, and that's in a community where income has not increased all that much. Almost everybody will tell you that they are giving more because now they understand what they get for their money."

Can the church do any less than let people know where the money goes? Accountability is a key element of faithful Christian stewardship. The accountability extends not just to God, but to one another in the entire body of Christ. For many years, the church provided no accounting of how it managed its money. When there was money aplenty, the assumption was that everything was just fine. The implicit message to members of the church has been to trust the leadership of the congregation to use the money faithfully. Now, when funds are limited and requests are plentiful, there is a greater interest in how funds are managed and used.

Stewardship Defined as Money

I remember counseling a young couple who were having marital problems. Their difficulty was not simply that they fought, but that when they fought they said terrible things to each other that, once said, could not be taken back. We are experiencing a similar plight in the area of Christian stewardship. Stewardship has been linked intimately with money, and many people see them as synonymous. Many churches yoke stewardship and finance to form one committee. Other churches simply have finance committees "with responsibility for stewardship." In various and sundry ways, it has been communicated that money and stewardship are, at the very least, two sides of the same coin.

When stewardship is defined as nothing more than money, at least three negative results occur. First, people feel devalued. Second, other equally important aspects of Christian stewardship are neglected. Last, the focus of stewardship turns to the function of giving, rather than to illuminating our relationship with God. Ultimately, the emphasis on money prompts us to focus more on the need of the institutional church to receive than on the importance of giving to help the individual grow in relationship to God.

Money is a powerful determinant of position and place in our culture. We are painfully aware of the haves and have-nots in our world. For many people, self-worth is deeply tied to fiscal stature. Churches that focus on financial stewardship, to the exclusion of the larger context, run the risk of alienating people and causing the less economically endowed to feel that what they have to give is not really worth very much. Sermons on the widow's mite do little to allay the anxieties of church members who are admonished to give more, do better, try harder, and keep pledges current. Quarterly statements sent from the church do as much to make people feel guilty as they do to inspire faithful giving. Without intending to, the church often sends the message that a person is valued to the extent that he or she gives. In some cases, preferential treatment is extended to the largest givers of the congregation. While money might make the world go around, it can eventually force the church to grind to a halt. It is imperative that churches remember not to value people for their money, but to value people for who they are.

When people are truly valued as gifts from God, then the attention to Christian stewardship will be broad based. The church will be a gathering space where people come to learn how to manage all that God has placed in our care. We will discuss time management, spiritual giftedness, values, the ecology, our communities, our global village, and our relationships as well as the way we manage our finances and share our monetary resources. Too heavy a focus on money simply does not leave us adequate time to attend to the larger concerns of stewardship.

The reality for many of our churches is that finance is a snake lying across the road—we cannot continue to enjoy the journey and look to the horizon as long as the serpent interferes. Hence, the focus on money makes sense in the short run. We tell ourselves that as soon as we vanquish the snake, we will get on with the real business of the church. Once money is no longer a pressing concern, we will give mission and program the care they deserve. The problem with this line of reasoning is that there are more snakes waiting for us just ahead. The way to deal with the snakes on the road is to find a new way to go. The old pathways keep taking us to the next serpentine encounter. The reality in many churches is that they work diligently to emerge from one financial crisis just in time to confront the next one. This points to a basic law of successful church finance: The best way to get more money is to stop talking about money. Lack of adequate money is the *symptom*, not the *disease*. If a church is not receiving adequate monetary support, it indicates a crisis of faith, not of finance. The only way to conquer the financial hardships of the contemporary church is to get back to basics and teach authentic Christian stewardship. As people grow in their relationship to Jesus Christ, gain clarity about their identity as Christian stewards, and find their place in the body of Christ through their local congregation, their level of giving of time, talent, money, and energy will increase.

This is a critical lesson to learn as we enter the twenty-first century: Stewardship is primarily about our relationship with God, not with our local church. The church is a means to an end; it is an entry point, a contact point, to the body of Christ. Ideally, the church provides us with a community of believers in which we can join our gifts and desires synergistically with other people. Our place in a local congregation ensures that together we will be greater than the sum of our parts. A stewardship focus that is limited to money can never open people to the greater possibilities of true community in Christ. Money limits us, while true stewardship liberates us. When the word "stewardship" is spoken, it should excite and inspire people to reach for new possibilities and greater potential. As it is, when stewardship is mentioned, many people merely reach for their wallet or purse in a distinctly defensive manner.

This is not to say that stewardship does not *include* money. We would be grossly remiss in the church if we did not ask the question, "What does money have to do with my faith commitment?" (And conversely, "What does my faith commitment have to do with my relationship to money?") While stewardship is always much more than money, we should not delude ourselves into thinking that stewardship is less than money. Money is powerful. Many people define themselves and others in terms of money. If our hearts and souls are captivated by money, then we must address money in relationship to

Christian faith. As we enter the twenty-first century, money remains an incredibly awesome force for good or ill. If the church is to have a continued impact for good in the world, it will need money to do its work, but it must also offer a message that keeps money in proper perspective. Money, at its very best, is a means to a greater good.

Conclusion

Local church landscapes have changed dramatically in the last fifty years. The maps that define our funding practices, our budgeting practices, our pledging practices, our tithing practices, as well as the manner in which we receive offerings in worship, have not evolved to keep pace with these changes. In the time of Copernicus, change was hard because it was believed to be so dangerous. Off the edge of the existing maps lay demons with sharp teeth and claws. Today change is still difficult, but we are encouraged by the fact that adventurous and faithful pioneers have sailed the uncharted waters and have lived to tell their tales. New maps are being drawn, and it is safe to navigate new waters.

Holding fast to the old ways may feel safe, but this is where the real dangers lie. Outdated practices may look quaint to some and may be confusing to others; but more and more, they are viewed to be simply out of touch with reality. Newcomers will not have confidence in an institution so perplexed by the way the world really works. Functional stewardship practices designed to preserve the institution are the maps of generations past. Stewardship practices that help to define and delineate the identity of the congregation and the larger church are the maps of today. A significant shift is occurring from viewing the church as a cultural institution to experiencing the church as the incarnate body of Christ. The next three chapters will explore in detail the implications of shifting the focus to the growth of Christian believers and away from the need of the institution to maintain itself.

Questions for Reflection and Discussion

1. What are the "maps" our church has employed over the years? Where did they come from? What is our process for modifying our maps?

2. How do we preserve the traditions of our congregations without allowing them to become ruts?

3. How does our church receive new ideas and proposals? What are the determining factors for trying something new or different in our fellowship?

4. What are our financial stewardship maps? How do we fund or budget for ministry? How long have we done it this way? Where did these ideas come from? How did our church fund or budget for ministry prior to our current practices?

5. How well does our church tell the story of ministry and mission? In what ways might we improve our communication about where money goes and how it is used? In what ways can we be more accountable within the church, as well as within our own lives?

CHAPTER 3

The earth at the center:
The danger of displacing the Christ

he Book of Genesis recounts the six days of creation. Humankind—woman and man—capped off the greatest creative achievement of all time. God created the earth and separated the waters, set the greater and lesser lights in the heavens, made the planet green and lush, populated it with many wondrous creatures, and then placed the entire enterprise into the hands of *Homo sapiens*. For millennia, no one could question the preeminence of God's crowning glory, the earth. Our planet, above all others, received the attention and affection of God. It is only natural that earthlings should come to see themselves as the center of all creation.

Nicolaus Copernicus, as well as many great minds before and after him, questioned the rationality of a geocentric (earth-centered) model of creation. Never intending to discredit the church or dishonor God—for he was a deeply religious man—Copernicus merely offered evidence that presented an alternative understanding. In his journals, Copernicus acknowledged that a heliocentric (sun-centered) view of the galaxy in no way diminished the glory of creation or the centrality of the earth in God's affection. The church would hear none of it.

By the sixteenth century, the church had created a very specific and strictly hierarchical view of reality. All things had been created to support the earth, the earth to support humanity, humanity to produce the people of God, Jesus to redeem the people and establish the one, true church, and the institution of the church to preserve and protect the truth of God in Jesus Christ. The institutional church could not tolerate anything that even remotely unsettled the "orthodox" view of reality. While claiming that Copernicus and his colleagues were challenging the gospel and threatening God, the only thing threatened was the status quo.

It is understandable that the church confused its understanding of cosmic reality with the truth. For centuries, the church existed as the unchallenged authority in matters religious, political, and scientific. The

leaders in the church were not villainous in intent. They were merely trying to preserve what they truly believed was right, and just, and good.
There simply was no room for a different view.

It has taken the perspective of history to resolve the scientific conflict
of the sixteenth century. Now, a heliocentric system makes obvious sense,
but for those who existed in the midst of that paradigmatic change, there
was great emotional, psychological, and spiritual pain. It matters little that
Copernicus was right. The "removal" of the earth from the center of the
universe created shock waves that are still felt today. No change is easy,
but a complete reorientation can be devastating. It is only when doing
nothing causes more devastation than changing that change becomes
tolerable.

In this chapter, we call for a radical reorientation in our understanding
of Christian stewardship. Such a reorientation must begin with the question of what it means to be the church. Stewardship is not a program of
the church, but a way of understanding the church in relationship to
Christ. We are stewards, striving to honor and glorify God through everything we do. We will once more reflect on long-standing stewardship
practices, but in a new light. ■

The Church as Institution: Means or End?

Clergy and lay leaders from throughout the Midwest gathered to
talk about the church and to discuss their hopes for the future. Two
questions were posed to the body on the first night of the gathering:
"What is the church?" and "What is the church for?"

Answers ranged from the universal to the esoteric, from the
abstract to the concrete. The church is the people, the place where people find God, the place where we offer our worship, the body of
Christ, the light of the world, the city on the hill. The church is God's
living room, a filling station, an energizing battery, a center of healing
and hope. The church is a port in the storm, a sanctuary from evil, a
hospitality center where everyone is welcome. The church is a launch
pad, a docking station, a locker room, and a kitchen for everlasting
nourishment.

When the emphasis shifted to what the church is for, the answers
were similarly diverse: the church is to save the world, feed the hun-
gry, make disciples of Jesus Christ, give hope to the hopeless, give
light to the world. It embodies Christ in and for the world, celebrates
the sacraments, prays, worships, teaches, and cares. It reaches out,
welcomes in, transforms, reforms, and informs. The church serves,

shares, loves, and gives. The answers could fill a book. It is striking that at no time during this exercise, or wherever else it has been shared, did anyone mention the functional work of organization within the church. No one said that the church comprises committees, or boards, or agencies, or task forces, or councils. No one described the church as the place where everyone serves the institution. And yet, as one nonchurch observer noted about his brother's church, "They spend more time in meetings than they do in worship. To me, it looks just like any other organization." This might seem to be an unfair indictment of the church, but before we dismiss the comment out of hand, it is worth mining for the good it might yield.

For the church to be the church and to do the work it needs to do, it requires some form of organization. Over time, systems are designed that facilitate ministry within the church. If a system seems to work, there is little critical evaluation to explain *why* it works. The system itself becomes institutionalized, and modification is rare. At some point, the focus shifts from the prevailing system as a means to the end of accomplishing the work of the church to the system as an end in itself that must be maintained and managed. The people who support the institution are "plugged" into the system where they will fit. Instead of making sure the system fits the people, usually the people who do not fit the system are simply encouraged to stay on the fringes. The gifts and talents of individuals are viewed as resources of the institution rather than as resources for equipping the saints for ministry. The focus of stewardship in such a church is on the institution's need to receive in order to maintain itself, rather than on the need of people to give in order to develop and mature in their Christian faith. Stewardship becomes a program to be sold to the congregation instead of a process of growth and transformation.

Gifts, Giving, and Money

Each person has gifts to give. Some are material gifts, such as money or property. Some are intangible gifts, such as time or energy. Some are creative gifts such as artistic ability or specialized talent. All gifts are valuable and important both to the individuals and to the church. One symptom of a church that has allowed the focus of stewardship to drift inward is that the gift of money is valued more highly than other gifts. Even when time and talent are highlighted in conjunction with financial commitments, it is usually the money that is tallied, tracked, and reported upon. This communicates a very powerful message about what the institution values. In a day when many people have very little disposable income to channel through the church, it is a disservice to discount other kinds of giving.

Sarah G. is a young woman who loves her church. She gives not only of her money, but also of her valuable time, energy, enthusiasm, and talent. She has given service to her congregation's church school, nursery care, a variety of committees, the visitation program, and many other ministries. When her husband abandoned her and their three children a few years before, Sarah stopped coming to worship. The pastor visited Sarah to see what was keeping her from the church. After a number of excuses, Sarah came to the real reason. As a single mother, her finances were extremely tight, and she did not have the money she needed to fulfill her financial commitment to the church. In her heart, Sarah determined that if she could not put money in the plate, she could not rightly take her place in the pew.

Sitting with the financial secretary of the church, the pastor lamented the fact that a committed Christian like Sarah should exempt herself from worship simply because she faced financial hardship. Even without the ability to give money, Sarah provided more support and service to the congregation than most people who paid their pledges in full every week. Both the pastor and the financial secretary agreed that their church needed to find a way to communicate to the membership that the value of each person's giving was much greater than the amount of money placed in the offering plate. The Sarahs of our churches need never be ashamed that they cannot meet their financial pledges when what they give in time, energy, attitude, commitment, and service provides value beyond measure to the church's ministry.

At a gathering of clergy and lay leadership in the Southeastern Jurisdiction of The United Methodist Church, the question was asked, "Why is giving important?" Among the clergy present, the most common answer was, "The church cannot survive unless all give what they are able to." The number one answer among the laity was, "Giving makes us more like Jesus." These answers reflect the difference in perspective that clergy and laity hold in the church. Not only do these differing perspectives reflect the respective roles required of clergy and laity in the life of the church, they also show the deeply held personal convictions of these leaders. Clergy leaders are representatives of the institution as well as shepherds of the flock. They have a dual interest in preserving the institution to enable the mission and ministry of the church to continue and in leading the people of God as they grow in their faith and faithfulness. The primary interest of lay members is to grow personally in the Christian faith. The clergy perspective is more structural, while the lay perspective is more relational. This difference presents an opportunity as the focus of Christian stewardship shifts from the preservation of the institutional church to the building up of the body of Christ.

Barry S., a pastor from New York, laments: "I just hate heading the finance campaign each year. Each spring, the finance committee emphatically states how important it is that the pastor not be seen as the one who does the asking for funds. By fall, I preach the sermons, I explain the process, I underline how important it is to make a pledge, I report the results, I sign the letters, and so forth. I hate it. By late November, I feel like I ought to set up a sign on the corner and hold out a tin cup as my parishioners pass by. Why does it have to be such a struggle?"

The reason it is such a struggle is that we make it that way. Asking for money should be one of the easiest things we have to do in the church. Asking for time commitments, for contributions of gifts and special talents, and for service on committees and work teams should all be simple matters. What makes them difficult is that we do not ask as we ought. The rationale for giving that we communicate is based on what the church needs, not on why it is important for the giver to give. A quick look through the gospels at Jesus' interaction with the disciples shows that Jesus talked to the disciples about what they would do and why. There was always a compelling vision offered and a rationale for what it would mean to the disciples. Both the costs and the benefits were understood. The disciples were treated like a team whose giving was directly tied to their development as whole people. Giving was assumed; Jesus did not have to tell them that they ought to give or how much they should give. He merely modeled and instructed what the giving would look like. Jesus taught the disciples giving in order that they might become the people God intended them to be.

A fundamental problem may lie in the simple assumption that people know how to give. Where does giving get taught? At home? At school? At church? On television? How do children learn the concepts of sharing, charity, sacrifice, and service? Where do we encounter concepts such as tithing, alms giving, and offerings, aside from the church? The church has a great teaching task in the area of giving of gifts and resources.

Tithing provides a wonderful example of the need for intensive teaching, but it also illustrates what can happen when a concept of faith development and grace becomes corrupted as a tool for maintaining the institution. Most of us define a tithe as ten percent of our income (though gross or net income is a hotly contested topic) that is given in response to God. But does that entire ten percent have to go to the church? Is ten percent all that we are expected to give? Is two percent, given in love and faithfulness, not every bit as valuable as ten percent? Is a tithe not just an Old Testament legalism that does not really hold for Christians today?

When tithing is presented as a legalism that defines what we must do in order to be "good" Christians, it creates more problems than it solves. In the Methodist movement, John Wesley set tithing as the *minimum* standard of giving. His understanding was based on a commonly held interpretation of the Scripture in a time where inflation increased approximately one half of one percent each generation. It also reflected a reality in which the church was responsible for many services and ministries that are provided by government and independent businesses today. The needs have changed, the delivery systems have changed, and the economic realities have changed. What has not changed is tithing and what it means to a person in relationship with God.

The word *tithe* means "a tenth part." In church parlance, a tithe is defined as ten percent of a believer's income that he or she should give in response to God's providence, preferably through the church. Many people accept that definition without question. Others, however, balk at such a contrived and narrowly defined standard of monetary giving. Regardless of popular opinion, the concept of the tithe has survived almost 4,000 years of discussion and debate. Where did this concept for giving originate?

The first reference we have in Hebrew Scripture to a tithe is found in Genesis 14:20, where Abram promised Melchizedek to give God a tithe of everything that he received as spoils of war. While this is the first biblical reference, the way in which the tithe is spoken of indicates a cultural familiarity with the idea. Since the term is used without any explanation, we can assume that readers and hearers would have understood what was meant. Therefore, the term must have had a history even prior to its use in Hebrew Scripture.

Military historian William G. McGovern, in his book *Military Strategies of the Antiquities*,[8] traces the notion of the tithe to ancient Egypt. McGovern claims that in Egyptian numerology, the number ten was a sacred and powerful number. It was the number of wholeness and completion. Soldiers were models of perfection physically, mentally, and emotionally. To be a soldier in ancient Egypt implied that one was a "perfect ten." When warriors went into battle, it was believed that they could continue to fight until they had received injury to a tenth part (a tithe) of their being. Once "tithed," a soldier was made incomplete, injured to the point where he could no longer stand on his own feet to fight. His salvation became dependent upon another. The tithe was a point of no return. A warrior was still self-sufficient until he incurred injury to a tenth part of his being. Beyond that point, self-sufficiency ended. In religious observance, the tithe was a voluntary act of humility, symbolizing the need for the power of a deity to ensure a person's salvation. To tithe was to put oneself at risk, to give up control, to acknowledge neediness. For the Hebrew people, the tithe was a supreme act of faith that endorsed their belief that God would provide for them in time of need. Sacrificing the means to provide for oneself was viewed as folly by others outside the faith; but for the chosen people of God, it forged a link of interdependence. Through substantial sacrifice, the importance of community, the need to care for one another, and the importance of connection to God for providence and encouragement were paramount. Tithing was an act of placing oneself in a special relationship to God. It also served as a means of fortifying the community of believers and creating a cultural identity of solidarity.

The Hebrew people carried the "tenth part" definition of the tithe with them through the Exodus, even though—for them—the mystical numerological power of one-tenth did not hold the same meaning. Through time, the abstraction of a tenth part became the concrete legalism of ten percent. In our day, it is easy to see that for some people, two percent of their income places them in an interdependent relationship with God; while for others, giving even fifty to sixty percent of income would leave them securely self-sufficient.

Even employing a more traditional understanding of the tithe as a universal ten percent standard for giving, the Scripture challenges our use and understanding of the term. This passage from Deuteronomy alone should cause us to reevaluate our comprehension of the theory.

> Set apart a tithe of all the yield of your seed that is brought in yearly from the field. In the presence of the LORD your God, in the place that he will choose as a dwelling for his name, you shall eat the tithe of your grain, your wine, and your oil, as well as the firstlings of your herd and flock, so that you may learn to fear the LORD your God always. But if, when the LORD your God has blessed you, the distance is so great that you are unable to transport it, because the place where the LORD your God will choose to set his name is too far away from you, then you may turn it into money. With the money secure in hand, go to the place that the LORD your God will choose; spend

the money for whatever you wish—oxen, sheep, wine, strong drink, or whatever you desire. And you shall eat there in the presence of the LORD your God, you and your household rejoicing together. As for the Levites resident in your towns, do not neglect them, because they have no allotment or inheritance with you.

Every third year you shall bring out the full tithe of your produce for that year, and store it within your towns; the Levites, because they have no allotment or inheritance with you, as well as the resident aliens, the orphans, and the widows in your towns, may come and eat their fill so that the LORD your God may bless you in all the work that you undertake. *(Deuteronomy 14:22-29)*

In over thirty years in the church, I have never heard tithing spoken of in these terms. There is a simple answer for this. This passage from Deuteronomy does nothing to support or sustain the institutional church. It focuses specifically upon the individual's relationship to God and the faith community. The institutional religious center serves as a clearinghouse where the transactions take place. The act of tithing itself is a celebratory act in response to God's goodness, whereby the entire community—including strangers, visitors, and the dispossessed—benefits. In this passage, the tithe is God's way of throwing a party. What short-term and long-term benefits might the church reap if it took time to explore this understanding of tithing in depth? Paul tells us that the Lord loves a cheerful giver (2 Corinthians 9:7), and nothing inspires cheer more than a good party. We have focused on giving to the exclusion of an emphasis on joy. There is joy in giving; and the sooner we learn to communicate the joy rather than the obligation, the sooner we will begin to see changes in people's giving habits. Tithing primarily benefits the people of God; it benefits the institution only secondarily.

Despite what many believe, giving to the church is not a tax or membership fee. In the passage from 2 Corinthians referred to above, Paul reminds us that giving is a choice we make. Truly, Paul believes that all mature Christians will give, and give liberally, but there is no mandate to give. Giving develops with understanding (and greater understanding develops with giving) of an authentic relationship to God. In 2 Corinthians 9:8, Paul teaches that God gives abundantly that we might have more than enough to meet our own needs and share with others. Paul helps his audience better understand giving by first reminding them of what they have received.

Many people feel that they have very little to give. Money and time are precious and rare, talents are limited, knowledge is sketchy; therefore, people hold back, fearing that what they have is not enough. Very few families work from a budget, and even fewer have any training in personal finance or money management. Most people are even less proficient at time management. When asked about gifts for ministry, most people will express uncertainty about what they have to offer. How can people be expected to give liberally to their churches when they operate out of a mentality of scarcity rather than a secure sense of their abundant giftedness?

It is not unreasonable to state that giving begins with receiving and a clear understanding of what we have. God has blessed us individually with gifts and talents, with resources both personal and material, beyond our comprehension. Pooled with the gifts and resources of others in Christian community, amazing things can happen. As leaders in the church, we have a responsibility to help growing Christian disciples appreciate what God has given them. Through guidance and teaching, we help people to manage their gifts better. Once this seminal work has been done, we have the right to ask people to give, and we can expect that the giving will be significant. In the next chapter, we will explore how the church can create a system whereby the gifts, talents, and resources of the people of God can be discovered, developed, and deployed.

Conclusion

The institutional church is a means to an end. It exists to enable the mission and ministry of Jesus Christ to take place. It stands as a training and testing ground for disciples in formation. The committees, councils, task forces, and teams that compose the administrative organization of the local church exist to facilitate the work of the church, not to become the work of the church. When administrative function blinds us to the discipling ministry we are attempting to perform, we have lost our center.

The stewardship task of the church is to appreciate and manage *all* the precious resources that God has bestowed upon it. The function of the church is to design a system that moves all these marvelous resources, both human and material, through a transformation process that produces an incarnate presence in the community and world. To make a positive impact on the world, we must have the world central to our vision. If our shortsightedness focuses our attention on the maintenance of the local institution, then the impact on our community and world and on the lives of individual believers in our midst will be nominal.

The institutional church is not the center of the Christian universe. The body of Christ is the center, and a shift in perspective is needed if the church is to survive and thrive. When the attention of the institutional church is on itself, the real work of the church, the transformation of the world into the kingdom of God, will not get done. If, however, the attention of the church is on the people and on strengthening their relationship with God and their community in Christ, the church will grow, and the institutional church will flourish. In the days of Nicolaus Copernicus, the church established itself firmly at the center of the universe, crowning the earth, around which all things in creation revolved. The leaders of the sixteenth century church, holding fast to their geocentric views, lost credibility and—in the long run—forced a rift between spiritualists and rationalists that exists to this day. Denying the evidence of wrong focus cost the church of the sixteenth century dearly, and it may well do the same to the contemporary church as we cross the threshold of the twenty-first century.

Questions for Reflection and Discussion

1. What are some of the ways our church celebrates giving? How do we communicate joy in giving? How do we communicate obligation?

2. Where did we learn to give? How was giving taught by our churches when we were children? How is giving taught in our church now?

3. When giving is spoken of in our church, what specifically does it mean? Does our church seem to value one kind of giving over others?

4. In what ways does our church teach the need of the institution to receive? In what ways does our church teach the spiritual need of the giver to give?

CHAPTER 4

At home in the darkness:
What we do not know can *hurt us*

The universe that Copernicus proposed was not a new idea. Aristarchus of Samos developed a highly complex solar system theory seventeen hundred years before Copernicus. The solar system of Aristarchus was offered to solve many of the obvious contradictions that an earth-centered model presented. By the early sixth-century C.E. (common era), a heliocentric model of the universe was as commonly accepted as a geocentric model. It was the church that shifted the balance toward the geocentric model, when it decreed that nothing in Holy Scripture supported the theory of a solar system. According to the creation epic of Genesis, the earth was created first, then followed the greater and lesser lights; that is, the sun, the moon, and the stars. As the world plummeted into the Dark Ages, a papal edict was issued that "controlled" scientific inquiry through the time of Sir Isaac Newton: all knowledge and scientific discovery would fall in line with the revealed truth of Christian Scripture or it would be denounced as satanic. Anyone subscribing to teachings that could not be supported through biblical scrutiny would be guilty of heresy and would be put to death. All knowledge must be consistent with the teaching and belief put forth by the Christian church.

For almost one thousand years, the understanding of the cosmos was modeled after the Mosaic tabernacle of the Old Testament. The sky was a tent, tied at the four corners, and the stars were mere adornments on the canopy of heaven. Death was the only way a human being could hope to pierce the canopy of heaven and see the true realm of God. Beneath the earth was chaos, and each individual had the choice of aspiring to heaven through right belief (orthodoxy) or Hades through wrong belief (heresy). By God's grace, many brave men and women, including the likes of Nicolaus Copernicus, Galileo Galilei, Johannes Kepler, and Tycho Brahe, chose the perilous road of "heresy," and the ecclesial edict was repeatedly challenged. The earth was a sphere; other planets rotated and had satellites; the stars were unimaginably farther away from the earth than the church taught; and the sun was the true center of our system—one part of a much greater galaxy. No matter how vehemently the leaders of the sixteenth century church denied the findings of scientific scrutiny, more and more people came to believe that there was a different reality from the one offered by the church.

The great scientific minds of the Renaissance hotly debated many things, but on one thing they all agreed: science was not slave to the church, merely maintaining an insupportable fantasy. Science could unlock certain mysteries, and thereby challenge the church to make sense of the mystery. For too long, the church maintained its immutable posture by force and violence. Whenever truth threatened to undermine the authority of the church, it flexed its muscles and twisted the truth to fit its own view of reality. Church leaders were committed to maintaining reality as they understood and subscribed to it, and anyone who challenged that reality was considered a threat to the church and an enemy of God.

During the sixteenth century, universities and seminaries were exorbitantly funded to ensure that students would receive a "proper" and "true" education. The commitment of education in the 1500's was to develop a right-thinking breed of churchmen—women were still denied access to the Christian halls of higher learning in most of Europe—who would embrace the status quo and stand firm against the assaults of the heretics. Priests and theologians were trained to maintain the institution at all costs. The gifts and talents of individuals were means to an end: saving the church from the dangers of the secular culture. Once again, the church had lost its focus. In so doing, it had lost its center in Christ as well.

This chapter challenges church leaders to turn attention to the greatest resource of the church—the people, gifted by God. For too long, we have stumbled in a self-imposed darkness, trying faithfully to fulfill our Christian task without having a clear understanding of our gifts and resources for ministry. Ignorance of the gifts of the members of our congregations suboptimizes the potential for service and impairs our witness in the world. If we hope to move from darkness into light, it is imperative that we have knowledge of our God-given gifts and opportunities. ■

Two Views of Church Organization

Cheryl H. says, with some passion in her voice, that one of her least favorite pastoral functions is to serve as the chairperson of the nominations committee. "Our process goes something like this: Only about five of the people on the nominations committee show up for the meeting. We then make a list of all our committees, look at who goes off, look at who's left on, and then somebody asks, 'What about so-and-so? Do you think they'd do it?' We end up with the same people on the same committees year after year, sprinkling in a new person here or there. We tried a 'time and talent' survey this year, but it didn't really help. Some of my people serve on six different committees, and then they all complain that no one new ever gets involved. Nominations is for the birds!"

Fortunately, not every pastor feels this way. A nominations committee has the potential to be one of the most vital work groups we have in the church. It can be the conduit through which the gifts and resources of a congregation are channeled to participate in the mission and ministry of the church. The nominations committee provides a valuable ministry for developing disciples by helping to deploy ministers throughout the church. Why, then, do so many pastors feel that the nominations committee is a hassle?

Figure 2 provides a simple graphic to illustrate what the problem is for many nominations committees.

Two Views of Church Organization

Structure ➜ Mission/Vision ➜ Program ➜ People

People/Vision ➜ Mission ➜ Structure ➜ Program

FIGURE 2

The first view begins with the administrative structure of the church. In many churches, this means that all the committees, boards, and councils are in place, and that they have a fixed or ongoing mission/vision for ministry. From this mission/vision, the church has developed a menu of programs, services, and ministries. Annually, the nominations committee is handed the chore of "plugging" people into this system. Rosters are filled, quotas are met, and charge conference forms are filled in and signed. No wonder many pastors feel dissatisfied with the process. Plugging people into "slots" is not a means for empowering Christians for ministry, but it becomes commonplace when the focus of a congregation shifts from following Christ to maintaining the institution.

Think for a moment about the implications of beginning with a structure and program already in place. The apostle Paul writes in 1 Corinthians 12 that the body of Christ has many members, and all of the members serve different functions. All parts are unique; each part has a different function. What happens when a part comes along that does not fit the system? Once a structure is set firmly in place, it is very difficult to adapt to new parts. Church leaders and councils face a fundamental decision: "Do we expect everyone to fit our system, or do we design a system that accommodates different kinds of people?" Not everyone thinks, acts, speaks, or dreams in the same way. Not every Christian comes bearing the same gifts. Church councils, committees, and boards tend to develop unique, specific, and often narrow personalities over time that do not easily adapt to new faces, voices, or ideas.

Years ago, Ben and Jerry's Ice Cream makers wanted to create a new flavor. The underlying principle was that people want fun food, and that ice cream is just one medium by which what people really want can be delivered. One thing that people really want is chocolate, lots of chocolate. Not just weenie little chocolate chips, but chunks of rich, wonderful chocolate. The people at Ben and Jerry's wanted to deliver what people wanted: super chocolate chunk ice cream. Their basic problem was that none of their machinery could handle the chunks. Everything kept getting gummed up. They had a choice to make: Modify the chunks to fit their system, or modify their system to accommodate the chunks. For the Vermont ice cream kings, there was really only one choice. Through the inventiveness of their research and development team, a cottage-cheese maker was modified and super chocolate chunk ice cream became a reality.

In our churches, we encounter Christian "chunks" of different sizes and shapes all the time. What do we do with them? Do we get to know them and work with them to find their unique places in the body of Christ, or do we try to find places for them to fit into what already exists? Are we guilty of always trying to force some square-peg chunks into round-peg holes? Do we look at our existing committees and programs and try to manufacture a "pretty-good" fit?

Carl is a big bear of a man, standing six-foot eight and weighing just over three hundred pounds—all muscle. There is no doubt where Carl's heart is. Carl is an evangelist. Every Sunday, without fail, Carl brings at least three other people with him who rarely, if ever, attend worship. Carl is a wealthy man who spends over $2,000 each year on Bibles that he gives away to anyone who wants one. However, he claims that it is food, not Bibles, that makes him a successful witness. Everyone who comes to church with Carl gets taken to lunch afterward.

Carl burst onto the scene in a small, rural church in northern New Jersey and set the congregation on its collective ear. The church, literally, did not know what to do with a Carl. Almost every week, Carl proposed a new outreach program. Carl wanted to host dinners for the poor at no cost to them. Carl wanted to hold revivals. Carl wanted to go door-to-door and invite people to church. Carl wanted others at his new church home to come along with him. Carl wanted to do something great for Christ.

One Sunday morning, Carl stunned his congregation by bringing an entirely new kind of visitor to worship. Without the knowledge of the pastor or parishioners of the church, Carl had "worked a deal" with a nearby minimum security correctional facility. He had received permission to bring twenty-four inmates to church. As the processional hymn reached the start of the fourth verse, the sanctuary doors flew open. In walked Carl with a processional all his own: twenty-four men in leg-chains marching straight to the front three pews. Once the rattle of chains and the echo of organ music subsided, you could hear a pin drop. Less than one month later, Carl left his new congregation in search of another where his unique perspective on the church might find greater appreciation.

Carl illustrates what happens when a Christian "chunk" hits the "chip-making" machinery. Everything breaks down. This local church felt that there was no place for Carl, and Carl, sadly, realized that he did not fit in. Today, perhaps more than ever before, Carls are showing up in our pews by the thousands. People, young and old alike, are coming to the church with a very different understanding of what the church is and how it works. Sandy K. speaks for many when she laments: "I just keep looking for a place where I can be me. I want to be involved, but all I get asked to do are things I'm not interested in. I have attended five churches in the past year, and you know what? Not one church has taken any time to find out what I want to do. They only check to see what I'm willing to do for them."

Church systems that cannot adapt to change are obsolete by their very nature. A narrowly focused, fixed system cannot meet the needs and desires of a variety of people. Church leaders need to work to design a continually evolving, continually improving system. The church as the body of Christ is made up of many members. The Body cannot be defined until all the members are identified and joined together. This is the second model offered in Figure 2.

Here the focus is first on the *people* and *their* multifaceted visions of the mission and ministry of the church. As the human and material resources of a congregation are discovered and developed, a structure can be created to deploy these resources. Programs emerge that maximize the effectiveness of a community of faith to serve Christ. To do this, the time-honored tradition of spiritual gifts discovery needs to become a central function of each congregation.

Stewardship and Spiritual Gifts

While Jesus never spoke directly of the gifts of the Spirit in the way that the apostle Paul did, Jesus nevertheless clearly indicated that all people have unique gifts to offer to God. The parable of the talents in Matthew 25 illustrates this point. The master of the servants entrusted talents to their care "as each had ability." The original twelve apostles were a diverse and eclectic blend of personalities and talents. The "church" that Jesus envisioned was a relational fellowship where every person could use his or her gifts and talents to honor and serve God. This is essentially the same model that Paul speaks of whenever he teaches about spiritual gifts. Paul addresses the issue of spiritual giftedness on four occasions: Romans 12:6-8, 1 Corinthians 12:4-11, 1 Corinthians 12:28, and Ephesians 4:11. Paul identifies twenty distinct gifts of the Spirit.[9] These twenty gifts form the foundation upon which the church of Jesus Christ is to be built.

Stewards Discover Their Gifts

For individuals to be faithful in their discipleship, they must be empowered to discover and develop their spiritual gifts. Too often in our day, churches spend little or no time in gifts discovery, and members of the congregation question where they fit into the community of faith. Shelley T. reflects, "In my church, people get approached to serve on committees all the time and they ask, 'Why do you want me?' The only answer we give them is that we thought they might like it, or we thought they might be good at it. We never really ask a person to serve because we *know* that he or she has the gifts needed to be effective."

What happens in a local congregation when people lack understanding about the spiritual gifts and talents of the leadership? Usually, the human and material resources are suboptimized, people expend a lot of energy and effort for limited results, frustration builds, and committee work becomes a chore instead of an exciting ministry. Tom T., following a spiritual gifts discovery workshop in Tulsa, Oklahoma, claimed: "All these years I've been a square-peg missionary in a round-hole teaching church. I always thought everyone else had a narrow view of what the church should be doing. Somehow I always knew that where I was wasn't where I ought to be. I served on a bunch of committees that had mostly nothing to do with my spiritual gifts, and I felt like I didn't belong. I wish I had done this [workshop] years ago. I think I would have found my place, and I would not have tried so hard to be something I'm not."

Spiritual gifts discovery enables people to be who God made them and gifted them to be. It also allows entire congregations to reexamine who they are and who God calls them to be. Spiritual gifts discovery helps people examine themselves in relation to the larger community of faith; but most important, it helps people better understand what it means to be a gifted Christian, seven days a week. The gifts of the Spirit are not given merely to provide support for the institutional church, though they have most often been explored in this light. Spiritually gifted individuals are the building blocks of the incarnate church that exists everywhere in the world. The church is not a place, but a people. The gifts of individuals are the means by which men and women can serve the Lord. Many people are confused about what their gifts are and what God's plan for their lives might be. Linda P. remarked that discovering her spiritual gifts helped her "get a handle on what God wants [from me]." It is difficult to contribute gifts when we do not know what we have to offer. The Institute for Christian Spirituality in Rye, New York, reports that only four percent of all laypeople and approximately seven percent of all clergy have a clear understanding of their gifts for ministry. How can we expect our churches to be effective in ministry when we do not have a clear sense of our potential for ministry within our community of faith?

At a leadership training event, each member of the administrative council and board of trustees was instructed to bring a Bible, something to write on, something to write with, and his or her favorite tool. After everyone arrived, each person showed the tool he or she chose. Some brought drills and hammers; some brought mops and brooms. One woman brought her laptop computer, and one man drove his garden tractor to the meeting. One person even brought a telephone.

The pastor of the congregation told the group that before they got to the meat of the meeting, everyone was to take his or her tool and do something outside the church building to beautify the grounds. Those who brought lawn equipment were pleased and went right to work. Some people modified their tools to allow them to participate, while others simply sat down and watched. After half an hour, everyone reconvened and told how they felt about the exercise. Those who brought appropriate tools felt very good that they had been able to contribute. The few who used their tools in creative ways said that it was difficult and awkward, but they had fun. Those who brought totally inappropriate tools felt frustrated and left out. They expressed feelings of boredom, anger, alienation, or stupidity. They felt that they did not belong.

When we design our church systems before we assess our human and material resources for ministry, and when we target specific jobs and ministries without first taking into consideration the diversity of our gifts and tools, we run the risk of alienating and ostracizing a significant number of people. As we strengthen our commitment toward racial and gender inclusiveness, we need to strive to make our churches gift inclusive as well.

Another area for special care is the way we define the gifts in our congregations. Not every person will manifest the same gift in the same way. When we talk about leadership or evangelism or healing, it is important to keep an open mind and a broad focus on what we really mean. This point was graphically illustrated for me when I conducted a congregational assessment of the Dreighton United Methodist Church.

Forty-one elected church leaders and their pastors attended a three-day workshop on spiritual giftedness, leadership interaction styles, and spirituality types.[10] On Saturday morning, we talked about the results of the spiritual gifts survey that each person had filled out the day before. One woman, a gentle and soft-spoken member of the church named Gladys, had been silent through the first day-and-a-half of the workshop. She was the kind of person who is overlooked fairly easily. We formed a large circle and began speaking about the results of the survey. In turn, Gladys indicated that her two strongest gifts were teaching and leadership. The lay leader of the congregation guffawed at Gladys's statement, saying, "Gladys, a teacher? You wouldn't catch her in front of a group of people teaching for anything. And a leader? Gladys is the consummate follower!" Everyone in the room burst into warm, friendly laughter. Gladys just smiled.

Immediately, one woman spoke up. "You know, I was new to the administrative council last year, and I didn't have the slightest idea what I was supposed to do. Gladys sat with me for more than ninety minutes and explained everything to me. She gave me a thorough explanation not only of our church, but of the whole United Methodist Church. I remember just about everything she told me."

A young man remembered, "My wife and I came from a

Lutheran Church. We didn't have the slightest idea what made Methodists Methodist. Gladys came to our home and talked with us for a long time."

Another woman chimed in, "When we had the quilting group for the craft fair, it was Gladys who taught me how to attach the squares and stuff batting."

One by one, every single person at the table recalled a time when Gladys had taught him or her something, and it was commonly agreed that whatever Gladys taught was retained by the learner. As one person stated, "She just has the knack for getting the message across." One might say, Gladys has the "gift."

As this conversation subsided, the chairperson of the board of trustees leaned back and said: "You know, it very well may be that Gladys is the most powerful person in this entire congregation. Think about it for a minute. Gladys rarely votes until everyone else has cast a ballot. Whenever there is a debate, Gladys waits until someone asks her opinion; and when she does speak, she often sways somebody else's vote. I can't remember the last time that there was a tie vote where Gladys didn't cast the deciding tally. Gladys gets her way more often than anyone else I can think of!"

Gladys just beamed. The moment was an epiphany for the leadership of Dreighton United Methodist Church. A long and fruitful discussion ensued on the different ways that spiritual gifts could be manifested in the lives of the members of the congregation. Some people lead from the front, while others lead from the rear. Some people teach in front of a class, some teach one-on-one. Some evangelists travel door to door, while others broadcast a powerful witness through the way they live their lives. Not all gifts look the same. Not all tools are used in the same way. Once more, it is vital to focus on the people who make up the community of faith instead of on the institution to which they belong. This is a radical shift for many of today's churches.

It has not been our practice to focus on the gifts of our constituency. A more standard practice has been to fill the slots on our charge conference forms, then decide what we can do to fulfill our mission as The United Methodist Church. This misdirection of attention leads to fatigue, burnout, frustration, and, in time, to a defeatist attitude. People can serve in only so many capacities before they stop feeling satisfied and productive. Margaret K., organist, choir director, pastor-parish relations committee chairperson, worship and finance committee member of the 800-member Dreighton United Methodist Church remarks: "Each year I think, 'This is it. I'm tired, I'm fed up, and I just don't have the energy anymore. It's time for someone else to step forward.' Then, I sign on for another year and find myself in the same fix. The thing is, I love my church, and I want to give anything I've got to make it strong, but I just wish what I did made a bigger difference."

Giving what we have to make a difference: This is what most people want. Giving what God has gifted us with for the betterment of the community of faith is the essence of Christian stewardship. It is poor stewardship to misuse, underuse, or just plain waste the gifts of the people who connect with our churches. Faithful stewardship at the congregational level means assisting individuals to find a place in the body of Christ where their gifts and resources can be most effectively and efficiently used. When the leaders of a congregation take seriously the role of connecting the human and material resources of the church with its mission and ministry, amazing things can happen.

One church in the Easton, Pennsylvania, area found new life through the exploration of the gifts of the Spirit. As an unusual ex-urban congregation, this small church had no money problems whatsoever. Its main problem was growth. For a full generation, departures exceeded new-member gains by a three-to-one margin. In 1975, the membership stood just above 400. By 1995, the membership had decreased to 148. Throughout the years of decline, the ministry of education for children and adults remained strong. Average weekly attendance in the children's church school program held at 60; while the adults averaged 45, spread across four classes. Each summer, the church hosted more than 200 children for vacation Bible school. Teachers and teaching assistants were never hard to find. The entire congregation loved children and learning, and it showed. Still, the church leaders were desperate to find some way to stem the outward flow of members.

Following a consultation with the district superintendent, the church made a commitment to work harder in the areas of local missions and evangelism. These two ministries were overlooked regularly in the planning of church programs and missions. As often happens, the church council responded to the new tasks in the usual Methodist manner: They formed a missions committee and an evangelism committee; thus, they focused on structure and program instead of on people and vision. Chairpersons were appointed, and committees were created—made up of leaders who were already saddled with major responsibilities in other areas of the congregation. Nine months later, I received a call to help the leaders do a congregational leadership assessment profile.

The pastor related that the new committees were completely ineffective. Planning was laborious, meetings were poorly attended, people complained of being "burned out," and no one seemed to care much one way or another whether his or her committee accomplished anything. Adding insult to injury, some of the best teachers and most committed workers for Christian education began to slack off in their educational functions because they were now splitting their time among two or three committees.

A spiritual gifts discovery workshop revealed that the leaders of this small church were extremely strong in areas of knowledge, wisdom, discernment, teaching, faith, and shepherding. No one among the leaders scored high in areas of evangelism, apostleship, healing or compassion. I asked the leaders of the congregation, "Why are you wasting your gifts, attempting to do what God has obviously not gifted you to do? Why have you chosen to channel your valuable resources of time, energy, talent, and money into areas where you will be less effective than in Christian education?"

It is important to emphasize here that I in no way meant to imply that this church should not be engaged in missions, evangelism, or any other vital ministry. However, we do our congregations a great disservice when we continually push them to work hard in areas where they are ill-equipped to succeed. We target our weaknesses instead of our strengths. That is poor stewardship. An apocryphal story of Thomas Edison's youth recounts how a teacher once told the adolescent to stop wasting so much time studying science and work harder to bring his poor grades in English and geography up to the class standard. Many local churches and annual conferences fall into the same trap, attempting to compensate weaknesses rather than to emphasize and encourage the development of strengths.

My recommendation to the Easton congregation was to do away with the newly formed committees on missions and evangelism and to concentrate on reaching people by improving the already superior Christian education program. I encouraged the congregation to think of the church as a brick wall, each brick representing an area of spiritual giftedness. We randomly placed cardboard bricks on a table, until we had six rows of three bricks each. I asked one of the participants to remove all the bricks that were not listed among the primary or secondary gifts of the leadership team. The result was something like this:

Apostleship		Wisdom		Service
Teaching		Evangelism		Compassion
Working Miracles		Shepherding		Faith
Helping		Exhortation		Knowledge
Discernment		Healing		Prophecy
Giving		Leadership		Administration
Christ, the Cornerstone				

FIGURE 3

Figure 3 illustrates clearly that the wall has no structural integrity. This wall cannot possibly stand with so many gaps caused by missing bricks. Is it not a better idea to tear down the rubble and begin again, building a strong foundation for ministry by using the bricks that are present? Does it not make more sense to work with what we have to create a strong ministry, rather than to expend so much time and effort lamenting and chasing what we lack? This does not mean that we do not concern ourselves with ministries for which we are not suited, but that we begin with our strengths to establish a foundation from which to grow in new areas of ministry. The new model for this small Pennsylvania fellowship looked like this:

Administration		Giving	
Shepherding		Discernment	Faith
Wisdom		Knowledge	Teaching
Christ, the Cornerstone			

FIGURE 4

Just as no one individual possesses all the gifts of the Spirit, it is unlikely that any leadership team of a local congregation will possess all the gifts for all areas of ministry, except perhaps in the largest of churches. Faithful stewardship means that we do the very best with what we have and that we do not waste time trying to figure out how to compensate for the gifts and talents we lack. Maximizing strengths is the best way for local congregations to exercise good stewardship.

The Easton church members began seriously asking how they might build on their strengths, not merely to improve their education ministries, but to grow as a community of faith. Together, the leaders of the congregation made a commitment to transform their church into a "Christian Learning Center, dedicated to offering quality educational opportunities seven days a week." Inspired by this declaration, the Easton church opened its doors to become a regional literacy center, teaching adults on Mondays—and children on Fridays—how to read and write. Each Tuesday and Thursday evening, professors and instructors from local colleges and universities offer seminars on a variety of topics. Retired adults pool their time and energy to supervise a latch-key program, where children and teenagers who have no one at home when they return from school can enjoy snacks and fellowship, do homework, and receive tutoring in a variety of subjects. A free daycare program for the children of single parents was developed, and a learning curriculum was established to make it more than just a baby-sitting service. Adult service opportunities scheduled on Saturday and Sunday evenings offered building and repair services.

The results? Within one year, the children's church school program grew from 50 children per week to well over 150. New adult classes have been formed, and weekly adult Sunday school attendance tops 100. Worship attendance has increased from about 75 to around 135 each week. A children's church program has been added, with a weekly attendance of approximately 50. Forty-one new members have joined the church, and only four have left—the first membership increase in 31 years. The perception in the community is that this is a church that cares, that wants to serve the needs of the people. Upon reflection, this congregation has become very successful in local missions and evangelism by making a conscious decision not to focus directly on either one. Instead, the focus is on faithfully employing the gifts that God has given them. Much more has been accomplished by providing a quality ministry of education than could have been imagined by either the missions or evangelism committees. Best of all, the members of the church have stopped complaining of burnout. Their fatigue and frustration have been replaced by enthusiasm and excitement at being honest-to-goodness, trustworthy Christian stewards.

Spiritual gifts discovery is not a "program" for the church to adopt. It is an *ongoing process* within the life of the congregation. At one level, the church does not exist apart from the giftedness of the fellowship of faith. Our gifts and calling define our congregations. Unless we understand our calling and our giftedness, it is impossible for us to be the church. It is a fundamental necessity that leaders of the institutional church make spiritual gifts discovery a priority. There is no finer way to empower people for ministry than to create a system by which gifts can be discovered, developed, and deployed in and through the church.

The method used to discern spiritual gifts is relatively unimportant. There are a wide variety of tools for spiritual gifts discovery, some much better than others.[11] Whether an inventory, survey, interview, or group exploration method is used, the key is to make spiritual gifts discovery available to everyone who is interested. It is especially useful with new members and seekers who come to see what the church is all about.

Stewards Develop Their Gifts

I recommend that spiritual gifts discovery become a regular part of leadership training in every local church. I also believe that spiritual gifts work with clergy and denominational leadership groups can provide enormous benefits. Spiritual gifts discovery work is an ongoing process, and we should review and reassess our gifts on a regular basis. Paul writes that gifts are not static, but they develop and change, and that by God's direction, the appropriate gifts will emerge as the community of faith has need. Beverly K. speaks of her thirty years as a lay leader as a "waltz through the gifts of the Spirit":

"When I was twenty, I wanted to teach so badly. I had never been trained as a teacher, and I had a very limited understanding of the Bible; but I really believed God wanted me to teach. I taught Sunday school for twelve years; then, when we had more than enough teachers, the desire kind of left me. Suddenly, I wanted to start visiting people in the hospital and nursing homes. I went to the pastor and asked him to take me around and teach me how to visit. Luckily, he was very open and very patient, and I still visit regularly today. Nine years ago, I felt God leading me to preach. I have never spoken publicly except to teach children's Sunday school. I thought it was silly to pursue preaching, especially since I live in a part of the South where women preachers still aren't accepted very well. Well, I preached twice and took lay speaker training. For the past seven years, I have preached at least twenty times each year. Just recently, I've begun to feel that God wants me to do something different. I feel that I want to do something completely different. My scores on my spiritual gifts test were very high in apostleship, evangelism, and compassion. You could have knocked me over with a feather! I feel as if the lights have come on. Everyone in my group thinks I would be a good missionary, and I think that may be what God wants me to do. We're going to pray about it as a group and see where it leads. I am so excited. You know, every time I have felt led by God to do something, I get excited all over again."

Beverly's testimony is a fine illustration of the way God moves us to ministry through the revelation of various gifts at various stages of our lives. As our context for ministry changes, so do our gifts and resources. The benefit of being "tuned in" to God for direction is that the excitement stays high. When we align our gifts, talents, energies, and resources with the will of God, a miraculous synergy can occur.

If there is a drawback to the process of spiritual gifts discovery as it has been used in the church in the past, it is that giftedness has been seen as a means to the end of filling committees for the work of the church. While the institutional church provides a valuable outlet for serving Jesus Christ, individuals are gifted to serve Christ in all aspects of their daily lives. We are gifted people to serve God, not merely to do "church work." A significant part of the process of spiritual gifts discovery is to assist people to apply their gifts throughout the week. What does it mean to be spiritually gifted as a prophet, or a teacher, or a shepherd at work? What are the implications of being a healer, or an administrator, or a giver at home? Is it possible to exercise the gift of serving, or leadership, or even evangelism when we are out driving the car or shopping? Just how far does our giftedness extend? The more we develop our gifts for use in our daily endeavors, the more effective we are in using those same gifts for the building up of the body of Christ. We are spiritually gifted people every minute of every day.

Just as individuals are gifted, so are congregations. The people who attend our churches are gifts to us. God is deeply interested in how we put these gifts to use. To underuse our corporate human potential is poor stewardship. Discovering gifts is only a first step in a larger process within the church. Rarely does God grant a gift in its full-blown perfection. There is much that we can do to develop and perfect our gifts. The twelve disciples that Jesus called were filled with the raw materials that Jesus knew would make them the foundation of the emerging church. No one would argue that the Twelve were at the peak of their performance in the early days. They were tested, challenged, taught, and tried. They "went to school" on the teachings, healings, miracles, and confrontations of Jesus. They stumbled, fell, flopped, got up, and tried again. Discipling is an arduous process that requires a great deal of commitment. The institutional church has an obligation to teach disciples how to use their gifts wisely and well.

A story is told of Helmut Thielicke, the great German theologian and professor of homiletics, visiting the church of one of his young preaching students. The young preacher blanched at the thought of preaching to his esteemed professor, but he stepped up to the pulpit and gave his best effort. Following the service, the young man waited for Dr. Thielicke to emerge from the church. Time passed, and the young man grew fretful and anxious. At last, his professor emerged, clasped his hand, and told the young preacher how gifted he was. The young man blushed and stumbled to respond to this great affirmation of his preaching ability. Sensing the young man's state of mind, Thielicke quickly spoke to correct the situation. He claimed, "I said you were gifted, I didn't say you were good."

Having a gift—and even understanding that we have a gift—says nothing about the ability to use the gift. Identifying gifts merely begins a process. The next step is to work within the fellowship to develop, improve, and perfect the use of our gifts. There is no way to determine how much time and effort is necessary to develop our gifts. In this work, we operate on God's timetable; but we can be assured that God will be faithful in supporting us in our gift development through the empowerment of the Holy Spirit.

Stewards Deploy Their Gifts

Still, even this is not enough. Tom C. remarks: "Spiritual gifts discovery is exciting, and I really want to learn how to use my gifts; but the church I'm in now doesn't give me any outlet for my gifts. I really believe that my music and my writing are talents that God has given me. I was amazed to find that I scored so highly on exhortation, prophecy, and teaching. My songs are my vehicle for using my spiritual gifts, but I don't think my church has sung a song written in the twentieth century yet. And everything is done to the organ. Who listens to organ music anymore? When I asked to play some of my songs in the church, I was told that it wasn't 'appropriate.' I feel even more frustrated now that I know what my gifts are and can't use them."

Deployment of our gifts is as important as discovery and development. Granted, deployment cannot, and should not, occur before gifts are discovered and adequately developed, but this makes it no less important. All of the most intentional and faithful work of spiritual gifts discovery and training to improve our gifts is worthless if there is no outlet for these gifts. A key function of stewardship leaders and church councils is to ask the pertinent question: "What should we do with the gifts we have been given?"

Yolanda P., a student pastor in California, remembers a time in the not-too-distant past when her congregation struggled to figure out what it should be doing. Through spiritual gifts work, the real problem came into focus. "We have a small church in an older section of town. Both the buildings and the people who live in them have been here forever. Most of these people came to church for an hour a week, and that was that. When I suggested we ought to do new things and start new programs, everyone looked at me like I was crazy. Anyway, we began looking at the gifts in the church. I thought the gifts would show that the men were 'putterers' and the women were 'sewers,' since that's all they ever seem to do. It was weird though. Sixteen people took the survey: Nine had the gift of service, and seven had the gift of compassion. Some of our secondary gifts were healing and miracles. We all scored the same! I began to ask, 'How can handymen and seamstresses use their spiritual gifts?' Then we heard about Habitat for Humanity. You can't believe what has happened. I used to lie awake nights figuring ways to get people involved, you know? Now I lie awake wondering if anyone will be in church on Sunday morning. They're all out building houses, sewing curtains, putting up wallpaper, and all the rest. Even when we don't have a Habitat project, we've got the 'Kingdom Builders,' a group of retired guys who will do fix-up projects for cost for anyone in the community who needs help. You would not believe it, but the members of this church are together all the time. It's wonderful!"

Bruce T., a member of Yolanda's church, adds, "No one ever helped us find the right thing for us to do before Yolanda came here. We all wanted to be kind and giving and do for others, but we didn't know how. We had the talent, we had the desire, but it took Pastor Yolanda to open the doors and show us how to do it."

We need pastors and lay leaders who can help us discern our gifts, help us develop those gifts, and then show us how to do it, opening the doors to be in mission and ministry, using the gifts and talents God has bestowed upon us. When our gifts are deployed in the world, the transforming work of the Spirit occurs, and the kingdom of God is experienced by all. This is the goal of spiritual gifts work.

Conclusion

When we shift our focus in ministry from the needs of the institution to survive to the needs of gifted Christians to be in right relationship to God through Jesus Christ, we need to be flexible. This brings us back to the Ben and Jerry's dilemma. As long as we take the unique gifts and talents of individuals and force them through a narrow and inappropriate system, we suboptimize our stewardship. The time has come to honor the gifts that God has given to God's people and to redesign our systems to maximize our potential as the body of Christ.

People who work on stewardship committees commonly ask, "What exactly should a stewardship committee do in the church?" I am not certain that there is a need for a stewardship committee, but a key focus for the development of Christian stewardship within the congregation is spiritual gifts discovery, development, and deployment. These are not three distinct functions, but three aspects of one process. This is a linear process. In order to *develop* our gifts, we must first *identify* these gifts. Before we can appropriately *deploy* our gifts, we must work diligently to *develop* them. It is important to keep in mind, however, that this linear process does not imply a distinct beginning and ending point. As we mature in our faith and move through various life stages and locations, our giftedness may change. God's Spirit moves where it will (John 3:8), and the process of spiritual gifts discovery is never ending. When we speak of a linear process, we simply mean that discovery precedes development, and development precedes deployment. At any point, though, new gifts may emerge, and older gifts may recede. This means that we continuously engage in the process of spiritual gifts discovery, development, and deployment in an ever-growing spiral.

In the sixteenth century, many church leaders were troubled that so many questions about the universe could not be answered using a geocentric model of creation. They were so convinced that their model was right—a model they had derived from the immutable Word of God—that they merely shrugged their shoulders and said, "Some mysteries are simply too great for the human mind to comprehend." Within a century, such a cavalier denial created a severe credibility problem from which the church has yet to recover. In our own day, the church struggles mightily to maintain its credibility. Whenever the church damages its credibility, support decreases.

Many churches are suffering from decline not only in membership, attendance, and financial giving, but also in enthusiasm and energy. Solutions to these problems are not evident to us under the current reality where the institution is central to all our administrative and organizational structures. Our structures have become so sacred that many leaders deny that they could possibly be the wrong structures. It may well be that our problems exist because we have chosen to focus on the wrong center. The church that focuses on its own survival is a church designed to fail. The church that focuses on relating people to Christ and to one another and to enabling people to discover, develop, and use their divinely granted gifts is a church designed to make disciples and transform the world.

When a church system for ministry begins with a focus on structure and then forces everyone through the system in the same way, it denies the unique, God-given giftedness of each individual. It is nearly impossible to connect people to the body of Christ in a meaningful way unless we understand who people are and what gifts they bring. If we look under the hood of an automobile, we quickly understand that all the parts are unique and that their effectiveness comes through their interconnections in the proper places. One part is not the same as the other. We cannot interchange the air filter with the distributor cap and say it does not matter. Only by understanding the function of each part and the proper interrelationships of the parts can we create an engine that will run efficiently. This is common sense. Why is it so hard to see this analogy in terms of the church? We take a uniquely gifted individual and say, "You can serve on the education committee or the missions committee or the finance committee . . . it does not really matter." Before we begin to put our systems for ministry together, our initial task is to identify all the parts and to strive to understand their functional interrelationships.

This is a fundamental shift. As one retired pastor remarked: "My ministry has been to work within an organization that expected people to serve it. It is encouraging to hear that The United Methodist Church is talking about creating an organization that serves the people to help them learn to serve God. I have often lamented that we moved God out of the center of what we were doing and that we have spent so much precious time examining ourselves. I will never forget one woman who joined a church to which I was appointed. She had a burning desire to care for people in need. She asked us to put her to work in ministry with the needy. We put her on a committee. After only two months she told us off by saying that while our world was dying for want of a savior, we made the selection of a copier lease our top priority. She didn't last long at that church. Far too often, we neglected to be sensitive to the needs of people while we took care of business. I'm glad that might be changing."

The change comes as churches focus more on the people and the God they serve and less on maintenance needs. The shift is dynamic. It means that we will no longer continue doing things the way "we have always done them."

Questions for Reflection and Discussion

1. What are my specific, God-given gifts for ministry? How do I use these gifts in my daily living? What am I doing to develop my gifts?

2. In what ways is our congregation gifted? What are our strengths and how do we build on them? Are we spending too much time focusing on our weaknesses?

3. Do we design our congregation so that it is open to the varied gifts of newcomers? Do we try to manipulate people to fit our system, or do we continually modify our system to maximize the potential of our fellowship?

C H A P T E R   5

The sun-centered scandal:
Change is hard, but the status quo can be deadly

icolaus Copernicus, and later Galileo Galilei, confronted an interesting argument set forth by the church in their day. When Copernicus published his model of a heliocentric universe, he was accused of promoting pagan sun worship. Some leaders in the church accused Copernicus of pantheism. Copernicus questioned in response whether it was any less pantheistic to insist that the earth must reside at the center of the universe. The church held the position that the earth was the crown jewel of God's creation, unique unto itself. All planets other than the earth were identical to one another, but inferior to the earth. The sun, while one of a kind, was simply a source of light and heat for the earth. The moon was a timekeeper, helping to mark months and seasons. All stars were identical, providing a canopy of light in the nighttime sky, shining from a flat plane at a fixed distance from the earth. Whenever Copernicus or any other astronomer pointed out a deviation, a comet or supernova, the church hierarchy dismissed it without explanation.

The church of the late 1500's was unwilling to entertain any theory that relegated the earth to a lesser position of importance. Disregarding any and all evidence to the contrary, the earth was considered the center of everything. All the stars, planets, the sun (it was yet unrealized that our sun was a star), the moon, and all other celestial entities were less important than the earth. All things in creation were made to support, adorn, and glorify the earth.

"There is but one truth." This is the pronouncement that Galileo and many others heard when they were summoned to appear before the Inquisition of the church. Indeed, the church left no alternative but to accept the narrow and simplistic view that it espoused. On June 22, 1633, after a brilliant career dedicated to bringing enlightenment to a world still lingering in the vestigial shadows of the Dark Ages, Galileo, age seventy, proclaimed:

> Therefore, desiring to remove from the minds of Your Eminences and of every faithful Christian this vehement suspicion, rightly conceived against me, with a sincere heart and unfeigned faith I abjure, and detest the above-mentioned errors and heresies, and in general each and every other error, heresy, and sect contrary to the Holy Church; and I swear that in the future I will never again say or assert, orally or in writing, anything which might cause a similar suspicion about me…[12]

Such was the power of the church. Such was the church's way of dealing with scientific discovery.

Centuries pass, but some practices stay the same. In the area of Christian stewardship, some practices continue—even when they defy logic or common sense. Just as it is obvious that all heavenly bodies are not identical, so it is clear that not all people who enter our churches are the same. The diversity is great, and it is growing greater all the time. How is it possible that one message, program, or theme will speak to this diversity? How effective is a church that communicates, "This is the truth, take it or leave it"? How do we hope to thrive in a new century unless we are willing to have open dialogue with the bearers of different ideas?

Stewardship in the church will require more and more customization. One size does not (nor did it ever) fit all. The work of Christian stewardship in a congregation is not to manipulate people to fall in line with the program. It is an empowering work that allows the unique and diverse relationships with God to synthesize into one flowing, evolving body of faith. Different ideas should not be feared. If the church has not learned this since the time of Galileo and Copernicus, it had better learn it soon. Chapter 5 offers a conceptual framework for viewing the diversity within the congregation, and it offers some insights into how we might use this framework to build more effective systems for ministry in our local churches. ■

Dave L., pastor of a small northeastern church, received a recommendation for a "can't miss" stewardship campaign. He took it to his finance committee and to the administrative council for endorsement. The response was very favorable. A committee was formed; the program was developed, implemented, and evaluated. Sixty-two percent of the congregation made pledges; there was an overall eight percent increase in estimates of giving; and the church faced a budget shortfall of approximately fifteen percent. While not bad statistics, these numbers are no better than average for what the church managed in the past. Laments Dave, "I really don't understand it. We work our tails off and get an eight percent increase; we do nothing and we get an eight percent increase. Why can't we break out of this rut we're in? Is there a better program we should use?"

The answer to that question is yes, and no. "Program" is not the right word. One financial stewardship program is pretty much like any other program. In the last few years, the quality of stewardship campaigns and materials has attained a high standard of excellence. The problem is not with the program, it is with the process. As stated earlier, a short-term campaign cannot do much to change the long-term behavior of members of a local congregation. Stewardship is not just what we do; it is the result of the decisions we make about who we really want to be. As we make a commitment to become better stewards, stewardship programs can help us on our journey, somewhat like stepping stones across a stream. Ultimately, stewardship is much more than the theme of any ten-week program.

There is another, more crucial reason why stewardship programs often yield results that leave us nonplused. Stewardship is a measure of our relationship with God. As Christian disciples, we learn a great deal about God, life, love, relationships, and faith. As Christian stewards, we take what we learn and put it into practice. The more we learn (discipleship), the more we can do (stewardship); and the more we do, the more we learn. The life of a Christian is defined by the tandem relationship of discipleship and stewardship. No one program can teach stewardship any more than a single program can teach discipleship. Both are lifelong processes that each person experiences differently. When a stewardship program/campaign is conducted in a congregation, at best it only speaks to the life experience of a small segment of its members. The saying, "Close only counts in horseshoes and hand grenades" applies here as well. Every congregation comprises a variety of people and personalities. The faith journeys of any given handful of pew-sitters on a Sunday morning will be very eclectic. A single stewardship sermon or a particular stewardship appeal has a limited audience. To communicate stewardship more effectively, it is important to understand the people who receive the message.

To put it another way, stewardship (as defined in Chapter 1) is the process of appreciating and managing the resources and opportunities for ministry given to us by God. The most valuable and important resources are people—gifted, passionate, visionary people who want their lives to make a difference in the world. No stewardship program will be successful unless it begins with a clear understanding of the people for whom it is designed. No church can manage its resources for ministry effectively until it takes seriously its greatest resource, the people. To help understand the congregation more fully, let us consider a conceptual framework—a Cosmology of Church Participation.

A Cosmology of Church Participation

In every congregation, there are a number of different levels of commitment and participation. To understand how different audiences receive and understand information from the church, we will discuss five different levels of church participation, designated by the cosmological titles: Solar Center, Inner Planets, Asteroid Belt, Outer Planets, and Lost in Space.

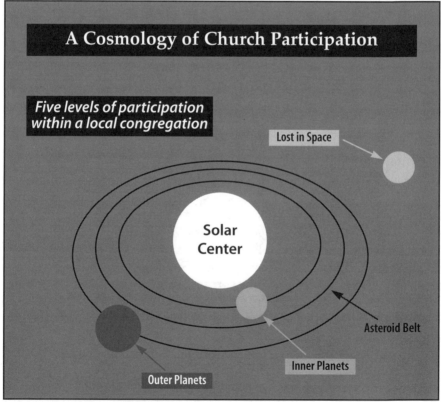

FIGURE 5

The Solar Center

The Solar Center of a congregation contains the ten to fifteen percent of the membership most committed to Christ and to the ministry of the community of faith. These people tend to be the strongest supporters of the institutional church. Metaphorically, they are the fuel that keeps the fire burning in the life-giving center of the church universe. They provide the heat and light. The Solar Center people accept a large responsibility for the ongoing mission and ministry of the church. They are the most faithful in their prayers, presence, gifts, and service. People of the Solar Center are continually striving to develop their faith by studying the Scripture, attending worship, participating in groups large and small, and by serving the congregation. These people make up the backbone of the church.

In most cases, prepackaged stewardship programs are not directed at this group. Most stewardship campaigns are designed to speak to both the seasoned Christian and to the novice to the faith. By trying to communicate to everyone equally, these campaigns often communicate effectively to no one. The people at the center of the congregation do not need a campaign or a theme. The people in this group need to be communicated with, one-on-one or in small groups. They need to invest themselves in planning the church's program, and they need to be encouraged and instructed in ways to invest their resources in the program. Lucien H., a retired investment broker, once said: "I listened to my friends and fellow Christians harp for months about the fact that we needed $8,000 to meet our budget. I just kept waiting. Everyone there knew I had the money. All I wanted was for someone to come out and ask me if I would give it. No one asked, but I ended up giving it anyway. I would do anything for my church. Anyone sitting at that table would do the same. I don't know why we pussyfoot around so often. We are so scared that we might offend someone that we do everything in our power to avoid talking about money."

Money is the new taboo in contemporary culture. On a recent television talk show, a panel of high-priced prostitutes discussed their plans to unionize. They were seeking a healthcare plan and collective bargaining powers! The spokeswoman for the group went on at great length about the kinds of services she performed on a regular basis. Her descriptions were both graphic and shocking. At one point in the program, questions were received from the audience. A young woman asked the leader of the group how much money she made in a year. With indignation and anger, the prostitute replied, "I don't talk about money in public; that's too personal!"

Money talk is also taboo in many of our congregations. Pastors and laity alike report that whenever money is mentioned, someone gets offended. It is interesting how rarely those complaints come from the members of the Solar Center. The highly committed church members do not get nearly as offended over money talk as the less involved members. Regular and sacrificial giving is a habit for the Solar Center. Learning to give sacrificially takes some people a lifetime. Many people never learn to give freely and generously.

The Solar Center is where the church can be most honest, where the truth can be spoken in love. There need be no sugar coating here. Some churches gather pledges from the Solar Center before they even begin talking with the rest of the congregation about giving. One church in the Appalachian Mountains struggled for years with a variety of annual funding campaigns. Nothing made much difference, and money was an ever-present concern. Upon making the decision not to go through the hassle of another financial stewardship campaign, members of the Solar Center of the church decided to start making their own commitments. They found that they completely covered their annual budget through the pledges they gathered around the tables of the administrative council and board of trustees. This for a church that in its seventy-eight year history had never once underwritten its budget through pledges. As the pastor explains, "We just never directly confronted the problem before. We always figured that if we could get the less-committed members to do more, then everything would be okay. We spent so much time trying to figure out how to get blood from a turnip that we neglected the plasma bank we were sitting in."

The Solar Center should not be viewed merely as the "cash cow" of the local church. More important than the money this group provides is the immense human potential for ministry. The time, effort, and energy of this group provide the momentum for the congregation. The spiritual gifts and talent pool of this company of people define the character and personality of a congregation. (Ordinarily, the pastoral leadership falls within the Solar Center. If it does not, watch out!) In most congregations, fully ninety percent of the leadership and support of the local church emerge from the Solar Center. As with our own solar system, the Solar Center provides the light and energy that sustain the life of the church.

Members of the Solar Center are the most likely audience to respond favorably to the process of spiritual gifts discovery. This group is also the most likely to derive the greatest benefit from what a spiritual gifts discovery process will reveal. In most cases, people who fall into the category of the Solar Center are deeply committed to faith formation and spiritual development. They willingly (or unwillingly sometimes) agree to accept leadership responsibility in the church because of their hunger for personal growth. Members of the Solar Center are the heart and soul of the local congregation, the living stones that build upon the cornerstone of Jesus Christ.

The Inner Planets

The group identified as the Inner Planets are the church "regulars." Faithful in their worship attendance, these people often show up for church school or Bible study, and they support the programs of the church. Even when they do not work at a church function, they usually attend to lend their moral (and fiscal) support. If asked, members of this circle will state that the church is very important to them. When pressed for more information, Inner Planets will explain church in terms of what they receive from it, rather than in terms of what they are enabled to give. Inner Planets understand the church as something they belong to, similar to a club, rather than as something they are a part of, such as a body. The depth of connection is not as great as that of the Solar Center. Still, they hold a strong allegiance to their particular congregation.

Inner Planets can be like a two-edged sword. Many long-time members hold on tightly to age-old traditions in the fellowship. Familiarity makes Inner Planets feel at home; therefore, they can be resistant to change. (Anyone can be resistant to change, but a large number of lay and clergy leaders concur that it is in this and in the Asteroid Belt level that they encounter the strongest opposition to change.) Jeff E. from New Jersey describes the Inner Planets of his church this way: "They have strong opinions about everything, but when it comes time to get down and dirty and do the hard work, they're nowhere to be found. They bend the ears of the Solar Center leaders with all kinds of complaints, and they even sway them from time to time; but you very rarely ever get them to commit to serve on committees or work teams. When things are going their way, you would hardly even know they're around; but boy, try to do something they don't like, and blam, they blow up."

By the same token, the Inner Planets, who make up approximately ten to fifteen percent of any given congregation, are the bread and butter of the local church. A majority of the church's programs and ministries are directed at this group. This segment of the congregation is faithful in attendance at worship and special church programs. While exercising a strong consumer mentality regarding the church, these people care deeply about the health and well-being of their church. They want the church to succeed, to thrive, and even to grow; however, they do not want growth to cause too much change, nor do they want the church's health to cost too much.

The majority of financial stewardship campaigns created in the past two decades target people at this level of association with the church. Most stewardship campaigns assume a basic understanding of the church and of the Christian faith, but not an extensive comprehension of either. Most explain in detail the rationale for giving to the church—something that is not as necessary with the Solar Center. However, the rationale does not always make sense to people with a more tenuous connection to the church. The practices encouraged by financial stewardship programs—tithing, pledging (or estimates of giving), praying for the success of the campaign, and so forth—have the greatest appeal to members of the Inner Planets. These concepts challenge Inner Planets to grow from where they are to a higher level of commitment and faith formation. Most prepackaged campaigns speak of practices already adopted by most of the Solar Center, but that are foreign to the commitment level of Inner Planets and beyond. While the Inner Planets are ready to be challenged, those farther out in the Cosmology do not relate to the invitation of most campaigns. The point is, most prepackaged financial stewardship programs that exist are aimed at only a slice of the entire congregational spectrum. Why we expect one-hundred percent response from programs that are designed for only twenty percent of a congregation defies reason.

Spiritual gifts discovery is important for this group to help individuals understand what it means to grow as Christian disciples. Most people in the Inner Planets group view spiritual gifts discovery as a personal exercise. The world view of an Inner Planet is more individualistic than that of a Solar Center. Inner Planets tend not to define themselves in terms of a community of faith, but in personal, private terms. The Inner Planet holds to the idea that his or her faith is just between "me and God." Spiritual gifts discovery is a wonderful way to help Inner Planets begin to see the need for connection within the fellowship. It challenges individualistic notions and can help prepare people to grow toward the Solar Center.

Bible study, church school, fellowship groups, and mission opportunities are very important to the growth of the Inner Planets. Each of these exercises offers an opportunity to help Inner Planets see a bigger picture. Bob G., a retired pastor, reflects: "In my last two churches, my good stewards were my Solar Center; my fledgling disciples were Inner Planets. My Inner Planets were learners, sponges soaking up everything the church had to offer them. My Solar Centers were my doers, very excited to put everything they learned into practice. I never made the connection between discipleship and stewardship before, but I see it very clearly now."

The Asteroid Belt

For most churches, about thirty percent of the people fall into this category. Jenny P., a young mother in Wichita, describes her association with her local church in this way, "We do church on Sunday, but nothing else." This is a pretty good definition of the Asteroid Belt: people who "do" church, but little else. These people attend worship fairly regularly, sing the hymns, pray the prayers. Some send their kids to church school. They toss in a few dollars from their pockets when the plate comes around, and they exit the sanctuary, having received their "God-fix" for the week.

This is not meant to be as harsh or as negative as it sounds. We need and want these people in our churches, and we are grateful to have them; but a church would not survive long based on the good-will and graces of the Asteroid Belt. For the vast majority of members in this category, the church is seen in the same way that a restaurant, a shop, or a theater is seen. They go to get what they want. If they get it, they go away satisfied. If they do not, they simply go away. For the most part, Asteroid Belt Christians believe that the church exists to serve their needs. They are not always comfortable when the church demands something in return.

The numerous informal polls I have conducted among pastors and lay leaders across the country all show that the Asteroid Belt members tend to be most offended by financial stewardship campaigns and requests for pledges. For the most part, people at this level of church commitment cannot conceive of a valid reason for the church to expect their support. Karen C., member of a small New York church, remarks, "Look, I always give something to the church when I go, but the idea of making a pledge is ridiculous. When I buy a pizza, I pay money. When I go to a movie, I pay for my ticket. I don't just haul off and send a few bucks to the pizza parlor or the movie house just because they need my money. Why should I pay the church when I don't go?" Sue S., a pastor-parish relations committee chairperson from Nebraska, says: "I'm embarrassed. That story you told (about Karen C.) was me just a few years ago. I thought it was outrageous that my church would send letters saying how important it was to keep up my pledge even when I didn't attend church. It used to make me so mad. Now I realize that I'm not really giving to the church, but

I'm giving to serve God and to participate in ministry through my church. That story really hits close to home." The story hits close to home for many people. At seminars, whenever I ask if participants have heard Karen C.'s comment or one similar to it, at least seventy-five percent of the people in the room raise a hand.

Most financial stewardship campaigns are not designed with the Asteroid Belt in mind. The campaigns aim at the people who are ninety percent "on board" with the church and with all that the church stands for. The majority of people in the Asteroid Belt report that they are not always clear about what their church does in mission or ministry, and they are suspicious of the way money gets spent. In many ways, people in the Asteroid Belt (and those farther from the Solar Center) are out of the communication loop in their local church. Many pastors protest that the Asteroid Belt members receive the same information as the rest of the congregation, but that is not always true. Word of mouth is the most effective means of communication. Bulletin announcements are effective when they are viewed numerous times and are reinforced through verbal announcements. Newsletters are read thoroughly by fewer than five percent of those who receive them, and they scanned by just another thirty percent. Judging by the numbers, it is probable that the newsletter communicates well with people who fall mostly into the Solar Center or Inner Planets' categories. If local churches want to improve the relationship they have with their Asteroid Belt members, then they must develop new, more personal means of communication.

Giving practices of the Asteroid Belt are on a "when-the-Spirit-moves" basis. These people do not usually give out of a sense of obligation or a desire to participate in the mission of the church, nor do they normally give out of a desire to grow as Christian disciples. Instead, they tend to give more to individual programs and appeals that interest them. Pledging to support a unified budget will most likely be something these people will never do (or never enjoy doing). Opportunities to support specific ministries or to extend relief and help to specific missional needs are received with greater enthusiasm. These people are very interested in the church—on their own terms. A common complaint of the Asteroid Belt Christian is that the church tries to tell him or her what to do, what to believe, or how to live. For many believers in the Asteroid Belt, the Christian faith is both personal and subjective.

Spiritual gifts discovery is a foreign concept to those in the Asteroid Belt and beyond. Mason M., a pastor in the Chicago area, reports: "When I did spiritual gifts discovery with my lay leadership, everything went fine; but when I held workshops open to the whole membership, I started hearing comments like, 'This is weird,' or, 'Why are we doing this far out stuff?' I realized that a lot of people in my congregation just aren't ready to examine their spiritual gifts."

I do not agree that people in the Asteroid Belt are not open to exploring the gifts of the Spirit, but I believe that many are not ready for such exploration because they still do not understand the need for having spiritual gifts. The majority of the members of the Asteroid Belt are "spectator Christians." They come to the church to enjoy the "show" and perhaps to receive some personal uplift. Once more, for Asteroid Belters, ministry is not something they understand as participatory, but as something provided for their benefit. To mix metaphors, Solar Center Christians are out on the playing field; Inner Planets are on the sidelines; and Asteroid Belts are in the stands. Asteroid Belt believers are not disinterested, but they are in a different relationship to the church than the other groups. Instead of treating all the groups alike, it is important to understand each particular relationship to the whole. Before spiritual gifts discovery can make sense to a member of the Asteroid Belt contingent, he or she needs to be seeking ways to strengthen his or her relationship to the body of Christ. This is a "lead-a-horse-to-water" situation. Until the Asteroid Belter experiences the thirst, he or she will not bother to drink. Margaret P., from Wichita, expresses her frustration with her own church in this way: "I need to be able to come to church to shut out the rest of the world, to step off the merry-go-round of my daily living. I need to be taken care of. I get very tired of people trying to get me to serve on committees, to work at church suppers, to tend the nursery, or to teach a class. All I ever hear is how important it is for me to take care of the needs of others. Well, my question is, 'Who is there to take care of my needs?'"

Margaret speaks for the Asteroid Belt. She loves her church, but she is at a very basic stage of understanding what the church is. It does not do any good to judge or berate the Margarets in our churches. Too often, we label this attitude as wrong, and we set out to make people who think this way see things from the perspective of the Solar Center. This is expecting too much. This needy attitude is no more wrong than a child's need for protection and nurture is wrong. It is a natural part of the development of a mature, healthy Christian. The church gains nothing by trying to force Asteroid Belt believers to "grow up." The goal of spiritual gifts discovery with members of the Asteroid Belt is to enable them to understand the many ways in which God has chosen to bless them. Help people feel good about the special gifts and talents they have received. Focus on what these people have received, not on what they ought to give. For many people, at all levels of the Cosmology of Church Participation, spiritual gifts discovery is going to open to them areas of giftedness that they have never perceived before. Just the process of discovery and discussion can begin to reorient individuals in their relationship with both God and the community of faith. The church best serves its own institutional purpose, as well as the larger purpose of discipling Christians, by adopting a developmental model with all levels of church involvement. The vision for many churches has been to make sure that all members act as if they were members of the Solar Center. It is better to help Solar Center Christians thrive and develop where they are and to work with all the rest of the people where they are to continually move into a more mature and dynamic relationship to Jesus Christ. If someone is, for a time, moving through the Asteroid Belt, then empower that person to be the best Asteroid Belt Christian he or she can be, while striving to instill in him or her an ever-growing hunger to mature in the Christian faith.

The Outer Planets

Actually, a better name for this group would be Comets. These are the Christmas and Easter Christians who show up from time to time. You can place the face, but you often forget the name. Every church has them, and changing the behavior of the Outer Planets group is very difficult. For this enclave, church is a "take-it-or-leave-it" proposition. Gwen C. speaks the mind of this group when she says: "Going to church really has nothing to do with how good a Christian you are. I learned a long time ago that I can be every bit as faithful on my own as I could ever be joined to a church. My relationship is with Christ alone; and for me, the church doesn't influence that relationship. Don't get me wrong; I'm glad that there is church for people who need it. I just don't happen to think it's very important."

The Outer Planets define the Christian faith in extremely subjective terms. Anyone familiar with the teachings of the New Testament knows that community, fellowship, outreach, and witness are key ingredients of the faith. None of these things can be accomplished on its own. Maturing in the Christian faith involves a process of moving from dependence to independence and then to interdependence. Far too many people retard their development by attaining independence of thought and faith and being content to stay there. For this group, Christian faith is personal and private. It is so personal and private, in fact, that these people often do not feel any need for a regular flow of input. Prayer, Bible reading, and faith-sharing are every bit as sporadic as church attendance. Since there is no perceived need, spiritual discipline and practice become optional.

Mike D., a recently born-again Christian from the Midwest, has a common Outer Planets story. "For the past twenty years or so, I would get on my suit on Christmas Eve and go with my family to church. I did it mainly for my wife and kids, though they didn't attend church much either. Church always struck me as dull and boring.

"I remember my mom making me go through a thirteen-week confirmation class back in the 1970's. I was glad when that stupid class finally ended and I was confirmed into the church. I remember thinking, 'I did it. I'm in. Now I don't have to go to church anymore. I've graduated.' I figured I knew everything I needed to learn and my ticket to heaven had been punched. Being the brilliant child I was, I knew that church had nothing to offer me. It was for geeks and freaks. I took my confirmation Bible, tossed it in my closet, and didn't step foot in church again until one of my buddies from college got married. I'm sure that the pastor at that wedding said some important things, but I was so drunk, I can't remember. Church was not a holy place or a special place to me then. I started going at Christmas just to impress my wife when I was dating her. I wanted her to think I was a cool, mature, stable kind of guy.

"Last year my wife left me and I fell apart. During the worst two months of my life, the only people who reached out to help me were three guys from work who are very involved in a program called Promise Keepers. They kept an eye on me, and talked to me, and really just offered me their friendship. They didn't preach at me, and they didn't try to ram the Bible down my throat. They just cared. They were there. As time went by, I thought, 'Jeez, I wish I could be like them.' I asked them one night at a restaurant, 'Why have you guys been so nice to me? What is it that you've got that I don't have?' That's when they shared their faith with me. It didn't sound boring, like I remember from when I was a kid. It made sense. I heard what they said, and I wanted it for myself. They helped me come to know Jesus. I cannot figure out why for so long I blew church off. If anyone had ever asked me, I would have said I was a Christian. I see now that being a Christian means more than just getting a confirmation certificate and putting in an annual appearance at church."

It is important to realize that the Outer Planets understand themselves to be faithful Christians. Most of the people in this category care about God and Jesus Christ, but they have defined the rules for membership in the body of Christ in their own unique way. Many of the Outer Planets people have negative feelings about the institutional church. They feel that the church has corrupted itself, that it has lost connection with what it was first intended to be. Rather than quickly dismissing these criticisms as the rationalizations of the malcontents, perhaps the church needs to listen carefully to the message beneath the message, to develop "ears to hear."

Stacy P., a doctor in Indiana, explains her avoidance of the church this way: "I go to the church seeking understanding of God's will, and I hear about apportionments. I go to the church seeking answers to life's hardest problems, and I get covered-dish suppers. I go to church seeking to find community, and I end up on a committee. I look to the church to model a higher standard of behavior, and I find gossip, backbiting, backstabbing, and bickering. After so long a time, I just got tired of looking and decided that the church couldn't give me what I was looking for. I still attend the 'big' services at Thanksgiving, Christmas, Easter, and Pentecost. I still love the prayers and the hymns. I read the Bible every day. I just don't want to get balled up in all the petty junk that goes on in the church."

Granted that this is an outsider's view that paints the picture in broad strokes, but much of what Stacy describes is a church that has lost its center. She speaks of a church that has focused more on institutional need than on the relationship of people to God and to one another. It is vital that we understand that much of what keeps some people from entering fully into the life of our local congregations may be valid criticism of what we have allowed the church to become. Not everyone who chooses to stay on the fringe does so because of a lack of Christian maturity.

Many of our requests for commitments of time, talent, and treasure are confusing to the Outer Planets. Outer Planets take for granted that the church simply exists. They do not question how a church plans, programs, or pays its bills. Obviously, someone does it; and they know they are not doing it, so why think too hard about it? The church exerts a gravitational pull, the Outer Planets swing with it; and that is just the way the universe works. This group tends to believe that if a church is in financial hardship, it is most likely because of mismanagement of funds. This opinion is not based on any evidence, but merely a conclusion drawn from the idea that churches do not need much money. When pressed to explain what respondents meant by the remark that churches do not need much money, Jim C. spoke for many when he said, "How much can it cost to run a business one day a week?"

This is the common view of the Outer Planets. Church happens on Sunday. The rest of the week is time off. In my first pastorate, I was repeatedly astonished when irregular attendees would stop to chat with me and ask what I did the rest of the week. People on the outer fringes of the church could not fathom that pastoring a church could be a full-time job. Kiddingly, some would say, "It must be nice to have a job where you only have to work one hour a week." Believe me, I just *loved* that joke.

Outer Planets have a very limited understanding of what the church is and does. The vast majority view the pastor as the paid professional who "runs" the church. Many are oblivious to the fact that a significant number of laypeople provide the backbone of the church leadership. Spiritual gifts discovery is a hard sell to this group. It does not speak their language. Outer Planets are locked in a one-on-one relationship with God that exists apart from the church. Spiritual giftedness has little meaning to people who are more focused on having God make sense of their lives for them. Tom C. recounts a story of his grown daughter, whom he had encouraged to take a spiritual gifts discovery survey. Patty attends church only when she visits her family at holidays. When she finished the survey, she found that her primary spiritual gift was shepherding. Her response to her father was, "How is shepherding going to help me get my life together? This test was a waste of time."

Many Outer Planets may feel that spiritual gifts discovery is a waste of time. In fact, it may be a wasted effort at this juncture in their journey of faith. In the orbit of the Outer Planets, it is much more important to help them awaken to the need for connectedness and interdependence. The Solar Center leaders have the opportunity to extend invitations to members of the Outer Planets to connect. Perhaps Sunday morning worship is not the best place for Outer Planets to enter. Traditional Sunday morning worship is not very interactive. Sermons tend to be monologues, prayers tend to be prepared and directed, songs tend to reflect traditions that are unfamiliar to newcomers or "rarecomers." Hence, few connections can be made. Seekers need dialogue: the chance to ask questions and discuss answers. Because Sunday worship has become so entrenched in our definition of "church," we may sometimes fail to *be the church* in more significant ways to people who stand on the fringe. Rather than attempting to understand our less active members, we often take the approach, "Why can't they be like we are?" It is a vicious cycle; insiders and outsiders looking at each other, shaking their heads, both asking, "What is the matter with them?"

The bottom line of a good stewardship program has nothing to do with the question, "How much will you give to the church?" It has everything to do with the question, "How are you doing in your relationship with Jesus Christ?" This is a critical distinction to make. Too often, we view each level of the Cosmology of Church Participation with regard to what it can give to the church. If we think in terms of the need of the giver to give in order to grow in his or her faith rather than in terms of the need of the institution to receive, then we realize that most financial stewardship programs do not apply to the Outer Planets—or to the next level—Lost in Space. They ask the wrong question. Outer Planets have made the decision, consciously or otherwise, that the church has little or nothing to give them. Why, then, should they feel any compulsion to give anything to the church? We should not be surprised that when we ask members of this group what they are willing to give, we often do not even receive a reply.

Lost in Space

Beyond the reaches of our galaxy, there is . . . space. We search the heavens, seeking once familiar faces who have seemingly been sucked into a black hole somewhere. We read through the membership records of our churches; and, by golly, there are more people on the official register than ever show up at church! In every church, a select handful (fistful? barrelful? truckload?) of people deem it unnecessary to ever darken the doorway of the sanctuary, let alone polish a pew by sitting in it for a while. We euphemistically call these people, the "inactives." The time has come to accept the fact that "inactive member" is a contradiction in terms, and it is a blemish on the reputation of any church.

Inactive members send a very clear message: it does not mean very much to be a member of this church. The church sends a very clear message to inactives: "You call the shots. You make the rules. You come, or not. You give, or not. You help, or not. It does not make any difference to us." In many denominations, there are no penalties involved, because we have confused being nice with being Christian. Peter K. says, "Why bother? I didn't attend church for sixteen years, and they still had me on the membership roles. I attended another church for five years, never joined, and received all the rights and privileges of everyone else. If the church hierarchy doesn't take membership anymore seriously than it does, why should I?" Strong words? Maybe Peter has a point.

We often claim that our inactives lack commitment. I beg to differ. I believe that inactives have made a commitment, and they are better at keeping theirs than we often are at keeping ours. Inactive members have sent the message that something is broken, something is not right. It is the responsibility of the leaders of every congregation to take steps to mend the broken relationship, or to assist the inactive member to form a new relationship somewhere else. In fact, it is more likely that an inactive person in one congregation will become active somewhere else than it is for that person to become active again in his or her present church. Either way, it is not an option just to leave someone hanging in the breeze. Churches are only strong when everyone participates.

When a person joins a fellowship, there are promises made on both sides. The church promises to provide welcome, direction, nurture, spiritual guidance, and an opportunity to serve Christ. The individual promises to uphold the church through prayers, presence, gifts, and service. What is often lacking is accountability. Who holds the church accountable for the promises it makes? Who holds the members accountable for their vows? Accountability is a key element of the stewardship function of a local church. Accountability is a shared responsibility of the entire community of faith. When someone breaks from the fold, it is everyone's responsibility to seek to bring him or her back, or to help the person find a place where he or she can connect.

I have often heard it said, in the heat of fall fundraising campaigns, that "if we could only find a way to get the inactives to give even a little, all our financial problems would be taken care of." Dream on. You have heard of getting blood from a turnip? Water from a stone? Those are easy compared to getting money from inactives. Asking for, and expecting, money from those Lost in Space is inappropriate and counterproductive. Many inactives complain that "the only time I ever hear from my church is when it wants my money!" Sadly, this is often true. Before the church has any right to ask for money, its leaders first need to make certain that they understand the condition of the relationship with the person asked. Nine times out of ten, there is a need for healing and understanding. Perry W., a pastor in Seattle, says: "When I visit someone in the hospital, I don't go looking for what they can give to the church. When I visit the prison, I don't go with my hand out. When I work at the soup kitchen, it isn't so I can collect from the people in line. In each case, I know that I am entering a situation where the people are in greater need than the church. Isn't the same true when we visit our inactive members? Don't we enter knowing that something is not right and that we need to be bearers of light rather than carriers of coffers?"

These questions are sound. When we adopt a financial stewardship program for our congregation, do we ever stop to think how the letters, bulletins, and sermons might be received by our inactive members? Is it our intention to "set them straight"? What if they are not crooked, but just distressed? No matter how carefully couched in biblical imagery or Christian symbolism, the message of many stewardship letters is downright offensive to those who have dropped out of the church.

Granted, not everyone who becomes inactive is a noble soul, wronged by the machinations of the institution. All the more reason to be very intentional about addressing inactivity as it arises. If someone has simply had it and he or she wants out, let us acquiesce to that wish. If he or she finds the current state of affairs in the (former) church unacceptable, then let us minister by finding him or her a new community in which he or she can worship and grow. And if there is brokenness that needs the healing love of Christ, then let us deal with it, and not let it fester into a lifelong infection that causes heartache for many. Let us develop the courage and bravery to be loving and firm. We have been nice too long. It is better to be Christian.

In regard to spiritual gifts discovery, ninety-five percent of all inactives are not ready to deal with it. Spiritual gifts discovery is a process within the life of the community of faith. Before we can truly help people discover their fundamental giftedness, we first need to do the preparatory work of connecting them with the fellowship. It is better to confront our Lost in Space members with a listening ear and an open mind than to go to them with an agenda or a program to deliver.

Conclusion

There was a politician who received an invitation to speak to the F.C.W. in town. F.C.W., in this man's experience, were the initials of the Federated Construction Workers. Because he was familiar with the organization, he did not bother to ask much about the group or what their concerns might be. The topic was "Change Readiness in a Complex World." The politician created what he considered to be a highly motivational speech on the trends in the construction industry and on how politicians and local construction concerns could work together to build a strong community. Pleased with his efforts, the man set out to make his speech. He arrived at the hotel where he was to speak and looked at the directory in the hotel lobby to find where the dinner was being held. Panic set in when he noticed that the big event was a Fellowship of Christian Working-Women (F.C.W.) in the ballroom. Somehow, he managed to get through the evening, but his memory of the event ranks as one of the worst in his political career.

This story stands as a parable for a prevalent situation in the church. Church leaders, figuring they know what they are talking about, assume that they know their audience. However, the focus of the church leadership has been upon the work and worries of the institution, rather than on the relationship of the people in the pews to God and to the fellowship. Assuming that they would find one audience, they are astonished to discover a variety of different audiences present. Yet they forge ahead, offering messages, programs, ministries, and meetings that may not be appropriate. In short, they do not know with whom they are working. They attempt to be in ministry without knowing the depth and breadth of their human and material resources. How can we as church leaders hope to create an effective system for ministry—and thus fulfill our stewardship responsibility to God—without first understanding the component parts?

There is no room in the church for a one-size-fits-all approach. Targeting one slender segment of our fellowship with a given program will always yield incomplete results. Why are we surprised when a program that targets the Inner Planets yields a poor response from the other strata of church involvement? Maybe we have not fully recognized the diversity of the target audiences in our congregations. Until we do, not much of what we do will yield the results we desire.

Kodak has long been a leader in photography. A number of years ago, it launched an advertising campaign to appeal to the broadest possible audience. Simple photographs with one single word appearing above them were run on black backgrounds in magazines. A picture of an older couple was titled "Memories." A photo of three teenagers, arm-in-arm, was titled "Friendship." A male college student kayaking on a fast-flowing river was titled "Action." A young couple bathed in candlelight was titled "Love." A mother watching her cherub ballerina perform was titled "Life." Kodak realized that different groups of people want pictures for different reasons. Instead of offering one photograph and saying, "Take it or leave it," Kodak looked to see where people were in their lives, and it met people there. Faith development is much the same. People are in relationship with God and/or a church for many different reasons. We cannot afford to hold up a single message or image before the people and say, "Take it or leave it." By listening to the people, getting to know people where they are, we can begin to recast the role of the church and connect more and more people to God in a meaningful way. The choice is clear: We may continue to treat everyone the same and wait for people to change to our way of thinking, or we may take seriously our commitment to Christian stewardship and strive to better understand people in order to foster a meeting of the minds and hearts.

Questions for Reflection and Discussion

1. How does the Cosmology of Church Participation fit into our experience of the church?

2. To which of the five levels of church participation are the majority of our church programs tailored? How can we expand our ministries to be more sensitive to and inclusive of the other levels?

3. How do we attempt to connect newcomers to our fellowship? Are we sensitive to the differences among different levels of commitment?

4. What are some concrete ways we can begin new conversations with each of the five levels of church participation?

The church's significance:
The mote in God's eye

 statement from an anonymous fifteenth-century monk reveals the position of the church of the sixteenth century: "I can tolerate any insult, save one, and that is insignificance." As long as the earth was the center of the universe and the church the "crown jewel" of the earth, humankind could boast significance. God revealed all truth to the faithful, and no other truth was acceptable. Ignorance was not an acceptable option. To know, to be right, to be significant were keen drivers for the leadership of the postmedieval church.

Yet, at some point, leaders within the church confused significance with greatness. Genesis 1 recounts the creation, which God called good— not great, not perfect, not best. It becomes apparent rather quickly throughout the biblical narrative that there is room for improving creation, and that humankind is responsible for contributing to that improvement process. When our first parents ate of the fruit of the tree of the knowledge of good and evil, their action proved to be both blessing and curse. They discovered that for every answer revealed, more questions emerged. Knowledge, truth, beauty, and life itself were not static, but ever changing, ever evolving. Repeatedly, the institutional church pushed to define reality once and for all. When Pilate challenged Jesus with the question, "What is truth?" Jesus remained profoundly quiet. The church of Jesus Christ has yet to grasp the significance of that silence fully.

For a century following the publication of *De Revolutionibus* by Copernicus, the church flatly refused to consider the teachers of the science of the heavens. Galileo renounced knowledge for "truth" under the extreme duress imposed by the church. When, at long last, the leaders of the church could no longer refute the avalanche of evidence for a solar system, they still could not relinquish their hold on their own significance. In an official decree, it was made clear that even though science indicated that the sun was the center of the galaxy, the church would hold fast in faith to the idea that the earth was the pinnacle of God's creative act and that the church itself was the crowning glory. Science and religion called an uneasy truce for a time. The challenges of Newton, Darwin, and Einstein lay in the future. Those were battles for another day. ■

Denial has been an enduring refuge for the institutional church. It is evident at all levels. Individuals within the church hold fast to ideas that defy common sense, because it is "the way things have always been done." Local churches lock themselves into self-defeating practices and defend them by labeling them "traditions." Annual conferences get swept up into administrative functions so completely that the facilitation of effective ministry throughout the conference devolves to secondary importance. The denomination turns its focus inward and strives to preserve itself, whether or not self-preservation best serves Christ. History reveals that whenever someone challenges these and other fiercely held positions, the church circles the wagons and adopts a defensive posture. Few individuals, churches, or conferences (and even fewer denominations) readily admit that there might be a problem. In the face of declining membership, attendance, and giving figures, the favorite practice is to work harder doing the things that yield less than favorable results. Now is a good time to admit that this just will not work. Working harder must give way to working smarter.

Nothing said about Christian stewardship in this book is new or innovative. I have simply held up each stewardship practice to an investigative lens to see whether it is based upon the call of Christ to make disciples or upon the call of the institutional church to preserve itself. At most, this book calls for a reorientation to the mission and ministry of the church.

To focus upon the survival of the institution is perhaps the quickest path to its demise. As Christ came not to be served, but to serve, so the church exists to serve Christ and the world. A thriving church is aligned with its reason for being. No church with an inward focus can faithfully fulfill the mandate to make disciples. For each of the stewardship practices discussed in this book and for any other you can think of, the first step to improvement is to ask, "Why do we do this?" That question, asked honestly, can do much to peel away the layers of self-interested activity in a local church, a conference, or an entire denomination. The question is well worth asking in relation to our worship, education, mission, evangelism, and other ministry practices.

In the sixteenth century, the church did an amazing job of defending its position at the center of God's creation. Repeatedly, over seventeen centuries, it warded off the revelations of science that challenged the geocentric view of reality. In so doing, it severely damaged its credibility in subsequent centuries. Could we not be doing the same damage today?

Scott T., a Baptist in Muncie, Indiana, reflects on the churches that he attended. "When I go to church, it's like I have stepped out of reality. The music is different, the language is different, the decorations are different. We are handed a bulletin that is more like an agenda than anything else. We sing songs that don't relate to my life at all. People act funny there. In my heart, I want to be there; I want to be close to God; and I think the church is the best place for that. But I really don't feel like I belong there. I get the distinct impression that the church is less interested in what it can do for me than in what I can do for it. I listen to the invitations to join committees, to work at dinners or on the grounds, or to give, give, give; and I keep asking myself, 'What's this got to do with God?'"

The church exists to help people understand what life has to do with God and what God has to do with life. The church can ill afford to be so enamored with its own image and identity that it forgets to connect the hearts of men and women, boys and girls to the love and spirit of Jesus Christ. Our universe is shifting. Reality is not what *we* want it to be, but what *God* made it to be. The church is not the center of the universe or the pinnacle of God's creation. We are the church, incarnate and continuously evolving. The institution is not the church, but it functions to serve the church.

God is the center. Joined in true fellowship with God and Jesus Christ, we generate the heat and light that gives life to the church. By the guidance of God's Holy Spirit, we extend the church into the world. All we do within the confines of a local church facility should move us toward this end. All other activity is poor stewardship.

The time, the place, and the opportunity are all ripe for effective ministry that will honor and glorify God. It is up to us to make the shift, to refocus on the true center. From this foundation, a vital and powerful ministry can be achieved, one that will one day win us the accolade from God, "Well done, good and faithful stewards."

The narrative budget

Budgets are tools that help financial leaders do their work in the church. They provide vital information for planning in the church. Budgets can enable congregational leaders to be faithful in their stewardship of the church's resources. What budgets cannot do, however, is motivate the majority of people to give. A surprisingly small percentage of the American population can read and understand a line-item budget. Too many churches pass out copies of the annual budget, believing that they have communicated important information. Upon closer examination, it becomes clear that very little communication has occurred. People do not give to budgets. They give less from the *head* than from the *heart*. People give to other *people*, to *needs*, to *causes*—to things that make them feel good and happy. Budgets miss these key targets.

Most of what is contained in a line-item budget is of little interest to the majority of people who attend our churches. Most people who are going to give to the church will give a certain amount to support the institution. People realize that there are costs to maintain the building, pay the insurance and utilities, and to support the pastor. They give to the mission and ministry of the church. If they are going to give anything more, the church needs to answer a basic question: "Give me one good reason why I should?"

The narrative budget is one way to give people a good reason. It focuses less on the numbers and more on what the numbers *accomplish*. It is a one- to two-page presentation that explains what the church hopes to accomplish and the funding needed to reach and exceed its goals. The following is an example of a narrative budget.

Anytown United Methodist Church
1997 Ministry Plan and Narrative Budget

Missions

The ministry group on missions has done an excellent job providing leadership for our congregation. Our mission involvement has increased greatly in the past three years. We support the local food bank and the soup kitchen in town, and we are beginning a second year with our thrift shop. The pregnancy center and drug rehabilitation center receive monthly offerings from our church. Through our Church World Service, Africa University, and Black College Fund apportionments, we give $3,500 in support; and we contribute approximately $1,200 to the six designated special Sunday offerings annually. We can continue this work next year with $6,000 in support. Our hope is that we can exceed that goal by another $1,000 in order to send a representative from our church on the district mission trip to Mexico in July. Future plans include reaching out to our community through literacy programs for children and adults and participation in the Women's Shelter Project. For an additional $2,000, we will be able to train crisis counselors to work with the shelter and to build a library to teach men, women, and children how to read. Your faithful support of these ministries through your financial contributions helps our church grow strong in missions and outreach.

Program

The church council has reviewed our program ministries for the past year and hopes to continue providing high quality opportunities for growth, learning, and worship in the year to come. In education, we fund our curriculum and resources with $1,500 each year. The additional $450 we received this year allowed us to purchase new commentaries and a set of Bible maps. We hope to do the same in the coming year, funding the church school needs and adding to our resource library. We need a television and VCR for the church school, and we hope to purchase the new *Disciple Bible Study* materials for a new group. We can accomplish these two things for an additional $1,500. We plan to purchase new whiteboards and bulletin boards for each classroom. We have received two donations toward our whiteboards totaling $550. With an additional $1000, we will be able to purchase these and the bulletin boards.

The worship ministry group would like to continue to count on $500 for the coming year for worship supplies. The $900 memorial gift allowed us to purchase new paraments for Lent, Easter, Christmas, and

Advent. We hope to purchase Pentecost and Kingdomtide paraments next year for an additional $450. We also plan to replace 50 hymnals. We have $200 designated for hymnals, but we need another $400.

The membership ministry group is still working on developing the Stephen's Ministries program, and we are thankful for the training we received this year. We hope that we can use $900 for training and resources in the church. For twenty-five percent more, the membership ministry group will purchase devotional booklets for distribution to homebound and hospitalized members and friends. We are still developing visitor packets and would like to purchase commemorative mugs to give to visitors to our church. These will cost about $350, and we will get them if the funding is available.

Pastoral Support

We have been very faithfully served and are grateful for the fine leadership of our pastor. The staff-parish relations committee has recommended a six percent increase in salary for the coming year that we joyously support. With increases in insurance, pension, social security, and travel expenses, the pastoral support for the coming year will be $66,975.

Other Staff and Salary

Youth pastor	$ 7,500
Secretary	$11,500
Music Ministries Director/Organist	$21,500
Custodian	$15,350

Building and Grounds

We estimate needs of $16,750 for the coming year. Insurance on the church and on the parsonage will be $11,175.

This is just a sample of what a narrative budget might contain and the way it might be presented. Dollar figures are round and easy to comprehend. No totals, and no bottom-line figures are provided. Instead, there are estimates of costs and dreams for what more might be done if money is available. Churches using narrative budgets note two things: (1) Few people, if any, ask for a line-item budget; (2) Giving to specific needs occurs more frequently. Narrative budgets do a better job of speaking a language that the majority of people can understand.

Notice three things about the narrative budget. First, it lists the programs and missions of the church first. Often, pastoral support, building maintenance, insurance, apportioned funds, and salaries are listed first in a line-item budget. One school of thought says that budgets should be organized from largest amounts to smallest. The sad reality in today's church is that mission and ministry budgets often come last because they are the smallest. What implicit message does this send? Mission and program budgets fund the work of the church. It is important to highlight these needs first. These programs and ministries are what most people care about deeply. We do ourselves a great favor when we list these things first.

Second, no paragraph lists only one figure, but a variety of figures: a low, a medium, and a high goal. The low figure is the minimum needed to do the work that must be done. The middle figure is a dream figure that would allow us to do more than the minimum. The high figure is also a dream figure that allows us to provide a vision for what we could do if money were no object. Many people who read a narrative budget are so inspired by the medium and high goals that they will "go the second mile" to make the dreams a reality.

Last, certain budget amounts receive no description. These are fixed costs, such as insurance, utilities, and maintenance that do little to motivate increased giving. Few people plan to give more than is needed to cover the fixed costs of running the institution. "Sell" the work of the church rather than the maintenance of the building and organization. These three things increase the appeal and effectiveness of the narrative budget over the traditional line-item budget.[13]

Spiritual gifts

he apostle Paul describes twenty spiritual gifts in letters to the churches at Corinth (1 Corinthians 12:4-11, 27-31), Rome (Romans 12:4-8), and Ephesus (Ephesians 4:11-13). These gifts defined for Paul the traits of the body of Christ. The lists vary from church to church, indicating that congregations are uniquely gifted just as individuals are.

An important aspect of the stewardship process in a local church is to discover the unique gifts of the fellowship so that all believers may fulfill their potential in the mission and ministry of Jesus Christ. Beyond discovering gifts, congregations serve Christ and their membership most faithfully when they create an environment where these gifts can be developed and perfected. The better we understand the gifts of the Spirit, the more faithful we will be in their management.

Below is a brief description of the twenty gifts of the Spirit proposed by the apostle Paul:

Administration. The gift of organizing human and material resources for the work of Christ, including the ability to plan and work with people to delegate responsibilities, track progress, and evaluate the effectiveness of procedures. Administrators attend to details, communicate effectively, and take as much pleasure in working behind the scenes as they do in standing in the spotlight.

Apostleship. The gift of spreading the gospel of Jesus Christ to other cultures and foreign lands. This is the missionary zeal that moves us from the familiar into uncharted territory to share the good news. Apostles embrace opportunities to learn foreign languages, visit other cultures, and go where people are who have not heard the Christian message. The United States of America is fast becoming a mission field of many languages and cultures. It is no longer necessary to cross an ocean to enter the mission field. Even across generations, we may find that we need to "speak other languages" just to communicate. Our mission field might be no farther than our own backyard.

Compassion. This gift is exceptional empathy with those in need that moves us to action. More than just concern, compassion demands that we share the suffering of others in order to connect the gospel truth with other realities of life. Compassion moves us beyond our comfort zones to offer practical, tangible aid to all God's children, regardless of the worthiness of the recipients or the response we receive for our service.

Discernment. This is the ability to separate truth from erroneous teachings and to rely on spiritual intuition to know what God is calling us to do. Discernment allows us to focus on what is truly important and to ignore that which deflects us from faithful obedience to God. Discernment aids us in knowing whom to listen to and whom to avoid.

Evangelism. This is the ability to share the gospel of Jesus Christ with those who have not heard it before or with those who have not yet made a decision for Christ. This gift is manifested in both one-on-one situations and in groups settings, large and small. It is an intimate relationship with another person or persons that requires the sharing of personal faith and a call for a response of faith to God.

Exhortation. This is the gift of exceptional encouragement. Exhorters see the silver lining in every cloud, offer a deep and inspiring hope to the fellowship, and look for and commend the best in everyone. Exhorters empower the community of faith to feel good about itself and to feel hopeful for the future. Exhorters are not concerned by appearances; they hold fast to what they know to be true and right and good.

Faith. More than just belief, faith is a gift that empowers an individual or a group to hold fast to its identity in Christ in the face of any challenge. The gift of faith enables believers to rise above pressures and problems that might otherwise cripple them. Faith is characterized by an unshakable trust in God to deliver on God's promises, no matter what. The gift of faith inspires those who might be tempted to give up to hold on.

Giving. Beyond the regular response of gratitude to God that all believers make, giving as a gift is the ability to use the resource of money to support the work of the body of Christ. Giving is the ability to manage money to the honor and glory of God. Givers can discern the best ways to put money to work, can understand the validity and practicality of appeals for funds, and can guide church leaders in the most faithful methods for managing the congregation's finances.

Healing. This is the gift of channeling God's healing powers into the lives of God's people. Physical, emotional, spiritual, and psychological healing are all ways that healers manifest this gift. Healers are prayerful, and they help people understand that healing is in the hands of God, that healing is often more than just erasing negative symptoms. Some of the most powerful healers display some of the most heartbreaking afflictions.

Helping. This is the gift of making sure that everything is ready for the work of Christ to occur. Helpers assist others to accomplish the mission and ministry of the church. These "unsung heroes" work behind the scenes and attend to details that others would rather not be bothered with. Helpers function faithfully, regardless of the credit or attention they receive. Helpers provide the framework upon which the ministry of the church is built.

Interpretation of tongues. (See Tongues.) This gift has two very different understandings: (1) The ability to interpret *foreign languages* without the necessity of formal study to communicate with those who have not heard the Christian message or (2) the ability to interpret the gift of tongues as a *secret prayer language* that communicates with God at a deep spiritual level. Both understandings are communal in nature: the first extends the good news into the world; the second strengthens the faith within the fellowship.

Knowledge. This is the gift of knowing the truth through faithful study of the Scripture and the human situation. Knowledge provides the information necessary for the transformation of the world and for-mation of the body of Christ. Those possessing this gift challenge the fellowship to improve itself through study, reading of the Scripture, discussions, and prayer.

Leadership. This is the gift of orchestrating the gifts and resources of others to achieve the mission and ministry of the church. Leaders move the community of faith toward a God-given vision of service, and they enable others to use their gifts to the very best of their abilities. Leaders are capable of creating synergy, whereby the community of faith accomplishes much more than its individual members could achieve on their own.

Miracle working. This gift enables the church to operate at a spiritual level that recognizes the miraculous work of God in the world. Miracle workers invoke God's power to accomplish that which appears impossible by worldly standards. Miracle workers remind the fellowship of the extraordinary nature of the ordinary world, thereby increasing faithfulness and trust in God. Miracle workers pray for God to work in the lives of others, and they feel no sense of surprise when their prayers are answered.

Prophecy. This is the gift of speaking the Word of God clearly and faithfully. Prophets allow God to speak through them to communicate the message that people most need to hear. While often unpopular, prophets are able to say what needs to be said because of the spiritual empowerment they receive. Prophets do not foretell the future, but proclaim God's future by revealing God's perspective on our current reality.

Service. This is the gift of serving the spiritual and material needs of other people within and beyond the local church. Servants understand their place in the body of Christ as giving comfort and aid to all who are in need. Servants look to the needs of others rather than focus on their own needs. To serve is to put faith into action; it is to treat others as if they were indeed Jesus Christ himself. The gift of service extends our Christian love into the world.

Shepherding. This is the gift of guidance. Shepherds nurture other Christians in the faith and provide a mentoring relationship to those who are new to the faith. Displaying an unusual spiritual maturity, shepherds share from their experience and learning to facilitate the spiritual growth and development of others. Shepherds take individuals under their care and walk with them on their spiritual journeys. Many shepherds provide spiritual direction and guidance to a wide variety of believers.

Teaching. This is the gift of bringing scriptural and spiritual truths to others. More than just teaching church school, teachers witness to the truth of Jesus Christ in a variety of ways, and they help others to understand the complex realities of the Christian faith. Teachers are revealers. They shine the light of understanding into the darkness of doubt and ignorance. They open people to new truths, and they challenge people to be more than they have been in the past.

Tongues. (See Interpretation of tongues.) This gift has two popular interpretations: (1) The ability to communicate the gospel to other people in a *foreign language* without the benefit of having studied said language (see Acts 2:4) or (2) the ability to speak to God in a secret, unknown *prayer language* that can only be understood by a person possessing the gift of interpretation. The gift of speaking in the language of another culture makes the gift of tongues valuable for spreading the gospel throughout the world; while the gift of speaking a secret prayer language offers the opportunity to build faithfulness within a community of faith.

Wisdom. This is the gift of translating life experience into spiritual truth and of seeing the application of scriptural truth to daily living. The wise in our fellowships offer balance and understanding that transcend reason. Wisdom applies a God-given common sense to our understanding of God's plan for the church. Wisdom helps the community of faith remain focused on the important work of the church, and it enables younger, less mature Christians to benefit from those who have been blessed by God to share deep truths.

All the gifts are given for the common good and the building up of the body of Christ. Gifts are not given for individual use, to confirm the truth of God to the individual, or to separate the spiritual from the unspiritual. The gifts are God's, as is the church. God bestows the spiritual gifts upon the fellowship so that the will of God might be done. To fulfill our role as Christian stewards faithfully, we must understand the gifts that we have been given.

Endnotes

1. Nicolaus Copernicus, "On the Revolutions of the Heavenly Spheres," Vol. 16, p. 506. Reprinted with permission from *Great Books of the Western World*, 1952, 1990 Encyclopedia Britannica, Inc.

2. Loren B. Mead. *The Once and Future Church: Reinventing the Congregation for a New Mission Frontier* (Washington, D.C.: Alban Institute, Inc., 1991).

3. An excellent introduction to key concepts of systems, quality, customer satisfaction, and process language is Dr. Ezra Earl Jones's book, *Quest for Quality in the Church: A New Paradigm* (Nashville: Discipleship Resources, 1993).

4. An exceptional resource to illuminate the plight of many mainline denominations' membership and funding situations is Ronald E. Vallet and Charles E. Zech's, *The Mainline Church's Funding Crisis* (Grand Rapids, Michigan: William B. Eerdmans Publishing Company, 1995).

5. Ezra Earl Jones, in *Quest for Quality in the Church: A New Paradigm* (Nashville: Discipleship Resources, 1993), defines the primary task of an organization as "what an organization must do in a particular environment at a particular time to carry out its basic mission and survive. . . . It is the basic work of the organization" (p. 28).

6. The 1996 General Conference of The United Methodist Church has taken great strides toward empowering churches for ministry. Many of the limiting suggestions concerning structure have been erased, and congregations are encouraged to structure themselves for ministry in the most effective and appropriate way possible. These decisions are essentially stewardship issues for local churches, offering freedom to use the gifts, talents, resources, and energies of each unique faith community to its best advantage. The General Conference acknowledges that change of existing structures is both good

and necessary, and it gives annual conferences and local churches the permission needed to change for the better.

7 A narrative budget is presented in Appendix 1.

8 William G. McGovern, *Military Strategies of the Antiquities* (New York: William H. Wise & Co., Inc., 1921), p. 447.

9 Administration, apostleship, compassion, discernment, evangelism, exhortation, faith, giving, healing, helping, interpretation of tongues, knowledge, leadership, miracle working, prophecy, service, shepherding, teaching, tongues, and wisdom. These gifts are defined in Appendix 2.

10 See Corinne Ware, *Discover Your Spiritual Type: A Guide to Individual and Congregational Growth* (Washington, D.C.: Alban Institute, Inc., 1994).

11 One disturbing trend in spiritual gifts discovery is a "proof-texting" process, where authors ask, "What gifts are needed in the church today?" and then turn to the Scripture to try to find the gift they want. The integrity of the Scripture is severely compromised by a disrespectful exegesis process. Warning: Beware of spiritual gifts discovery tools that feel compelled to add to the scriptural list.

12 *The Galileo Affair: A Documentary History*, ed. and trans. Maurice A. Finocchiaro (Berkeley, California: The Regents of the University of California, 1989), p. 292.

13 Note: the line-item budget is still a necessary and useful tool for the work of the financial leadership in the church. Use the tool to provide something appealing to the congregation. My brother-in-law is a butcher. I enjoy the work that he does by feasting at his table, not by looking at his tools. Think about it.

For further reading

The resources below will help as you seek to relate the concepts about Christian stewardship discussed in this book to the various aspects of your ministry.

Barrett, Wayne C. *The Church Finance Idea Book.* Nashville: Discipleship Resources, 1989.

Barrett, Wayne C. *More Money, New Money, Big Money: Creative Strategies for Funding Today's Church.* Nashville: Discipleship Resources, 1992.

Barrett, Wayne C. *Get Well! Stay Well! Prescriptions for a Financially Healthy Congregation.* Nashville: Discipleship Resources, 1997.

Dick, Dan R. *Choices & Challenges: Stewardship Strategies for Youth.* Nashville: Discipleship Resources, 1994.

Hall, Douglas John. *The Steward: A Biblical Symbol Come of Age.* Grand Rapids, Michigan: William B. Eerdmans Publishing Company, 1990.

Joiner, Donald W. *Christians & Money: A Guide to Personal Finance.* Nashville: Discipleship Resources, 1991.

Jones, Ezra E. *Quest for Quality in the Church: A New Paradigm.* Nashville: Discipleship Resources, 1993.

Jones, Ezra E. *Think About It: Reflections on Quality and The United Methodist Church.* Nashville: Discipleship Resources, 1996.

Mather, Herb. *Don't Shoot the Horse ('Til You Know How to Drive the Tractor).* Nashville: Discipleship Resources, 1994.

Mead, Loren B. *The Once and Future Church: Reinventing the Congregation for a New Mission Frontier.* Washington, D.C.: Alban Institute, Inc., 1991.

Miller, Herb. *Money ~~Isn't~~ Is Everything: What Jesus Said About the Spiritual Power of Money.* Nashville: Discipleship Resources, 1994.

Rusbuldt, Richard E. *A Workbook on Biblical Stewardship.* Grand Rapids, Michigan: William B. Eerdmans Publishing Company, 1994.

Wimberly, Norma. *Putting God First: The Tithe.* Nashville: Discipleship Resources, 1988.